Cut Flowers

T0046206

Celestina Robertson
Photography Salsabil Morrison

bloom
gardening · nature · inspiration

Contents

03

Grow / p56
Achieve an
abundant harvest
each season

04

Care / p126
Learn to condition
and arrange
your flowers

Introduction

It was the moment between six and seven when every flower – roses, carnations, irises, lilac – glows; white, violet, red, deep orange; every flower seems to burn by itself, softly, purely in the misty beds
Virginia Woolf, *Mrs Dalloway*

What is it about flowers that brings us so much joy? They have always played an intrinsic part in the key human celebrations of birth, marriage and death. Different blooms have a particular significance in cultures all over the world, from gifting posies of lily of the valley on May Day in France to the exchange of floral garlands between the bride and groom at Indian weddings. The cultural use of cut flowers connects us to a sense of time and place, to our ancestors and a shared history.

Flowers can evoke more than just a sense of happiness. The scent from a bloom like a sweet pea can stop us in our tracks and perhaps transport us to a different time and place. A request for a specific variety for wedding or sympathy flowers is often tied to a treasured memory of someone special in our lives.

Since the mid-20th century there has been huge growth in the floriculture industry worldwide. In countries associated with the global north, cut flowers have become a commodity, an everyday purchase rather than purely part of a special occasion. This global trade means that it is possible to buy a bunch of roses on any day of the year, with flowers grown and shipped from industrial-scale farms around the world on a daily basis. The rise of supermarket shopping means that cut flowers are on sale to a greater number of customers than ever before at relatively cheap prices.

Despite this wide availability of flowers, it feels like we have lost more than we've gained. In commercial floriculture, blooms are grown in industrial and often mechanised settings, with little connection to wildlife or to the natural world. Many varieties are grown in sterile, hydroponic systems and never touch the soil. There is a cocktail of chemicals present in the production chain through cultivation, post-harvest and transportation. New flower varieties have been bred for longer vase life and ease of transport, which often means sacrificing certain elements such as scent. In our fast-paced lives we have become used to having whatever we want, whenever we want it, but in this we have lost something precious; we've lost our connection to the seasons, to the natural world, and our sense of time and place.

There has been a real resurgence of interest in growing your own, whether it be vegetables or flowers. We want to grow nutritious food that doesn't have to travel huge distances to reach our plates, and in the same way we can raise seasonal flowers in the garden to fill our homes with colour and scent. We all know about the mental health benefits of spending time in the garden, and there is a genuine pleasure and satisfaction that comes from nurturing a plant from seed to fruition. Growing your own flowers for cutting is all about bringing the outside into the home, reconnecting with a sense of seasonality and nature. Flowers are food for the soul, and it's time to rediscover the beauty of blooms grown in tune with the seasons.

Opposite An early summer arrangement with *Alchemilla mollis* (lady's mantle), pittosporum foliage, astrantia, foxgloves, cornflowers, *Salvia nemorosa* 'Caradonna' (Balkan clary 'Caradonna') and polemonium

FOR THE LOVE OF CUT FLOWERS

I absolutely *love* flowers. But my love of flowers is about more than just the blooms themselves – it's about the whole start-to-end process, from sowing seed and growing plants right through to producing something beautiful for people to enjoy. It's so satisfying to nurture plants, to cut and gather armfuls of flowers that I've grown myself, and to know how much joy they will bring to others.

My horticultural journey started with work experience on organic farms in the UK where the ethos of growing was rooted in ecology and completely focused on supplying seasonal food to local people. Understanding food provenance and developing a relationship between the farmer and the customer wasn't the norm in the 1990s, but there were a growing number of small farms working hard to bring nutritious, organic food to a wider audience and to raise public awareness of harmful industrial growing processes and complex supply chains. To continue my horticultural education I enrolled at college to study garden design, which is where I met my husband. Garden design was the perfect marriage of my two loves – art and the garden – and I've always felt that creating a planting plan is like painting a space with plants. Little did I know then that a move from London to rural Norfolk would take me in a completely new horticultural direction.

FOREVER GREEN FLOWER COMPANY

I had always grown my own flowers alongside vegetables on an allotment, but bit by bit the flowers began to take over my plot! I started a search for land to rent in order to create a cut flower farm – my idea was to establish something along the lines of the organic farms I had worked on years before. I was aware of the environmental issues of imported flowers in the early days of my horticultural career and I knew about the damaging impact of their production and transportation. Others must have felt equally strongly about these issues, because at the time I started Forever Green Flower Company, a cut flower-growing movement was starting to establish itself in the UK, and small flower farms founded by artisan growers on small acreages were springing up across the country. Many of these growers were, and still are, dedicated to growing seasonal blooms in a sustainable, environmentally friendly way for their local communities, offering flowers that bring a more natural, garden-grown aesthetic to floral arrangements.

The UK once had a thriving flower industry that was still going until the 1980s when it was decimated by a number of factors, including the growth of global industry and the dominance of supermarkets. Only a fraction of commercial-scale flower farms remain, but the number of smaller-scale growers is increasing year on year, and demand for locally grown flowers is on the rise. Now I am part of a community of cut flower growers, many of whom centre social and environmental justice at the heart of their business, all of them supplying beautiful, seasonal blooms to flower lovers who don't want their purchases to cost the Earth.

01

Learn
Understand the makings of a perfect cut flower

Why grow your own flowers?

Why should anyone put in the time and effort to grow their own flowers when they are so readily available to buy? The wonderful thing about a global trade in cut flowers is that we can purchase them at any time of the year – we can fill our homes with colour or send a floral gift to a friend or relative, even in the depths of winter. But that global trade comes with more than just the cost of the flowers themselves – there is a social and environmental cost that we must also consider, as with all of the purchases that we make. Growing your own flowers is just one way to help make a difference.

The other undeniable reason for growing your own flowers is for the pure joy of it. It is a salve to our lost connection to seasonality and all of the pleasure that being in tune with the seasons brings. The natural world is a provider of inspiration, and growing and arranging seasonal flowers can result in the most beautifully considered combinations of flowers that you would never usually be able to purchase together.

A SUSTAINABLE CHOICE

Earth has seen a significant increase in greenhouse gas emissions which has led to a rapid warming of our atmosphere. The effects of climate change on our planet are all too evident: extreme weather events and years of record-breaking heat are creating challenging conditions for life across the globe. Yet our levels of consumption continue to rise, leading to widespread and well-documented environmental degradation.

The concept of sustainability is complex but is best defined by the UN as: 'development that meets the needs of the present without compromising the ability of future generations to meet the needs of their own'. Put simply, we need to consider

Above A garden-gathered bunch with astrantia, foxgloves and *Anemone* × *hybrida* (Japanese anemone) **Opposite** Astrantia in summer

how our actions today will have an impact on generations to come.

There are three pillars of sustainability – people, profit and planet – which comprise social and economic development, and environmental protection. When we make choices about the products we buy – cut flowers for instance, or items we purchase for use in the garden – we should question the provenance of that product and ask if the three pillars are equally and fairly represented. If a bouquet purchase is cheap at the point of sale it usually means that the cost is being paid elsewhere, with poorly paid farm labour for example, or a production process that is detrimental to workers' health or the natural environment.

There are many troubling issues with the commercial production of cut flowers and a number of social and environmental concerns have long been highlighted in the global floriculture industry. Cut flowers grown on an industrial scale and exported across the world have a considerable carbon footprint. The transportation of these blooms is just one small element of their impact, and we need to think about the entire production process of cut flowers, measuring both direct and indirect emissions. Here are just some of the factors that contribute to that high carbon footprint: artificial lighting,

heating or cooling of temperature-controlled glasshouse growing systems; automated production in greenhouses and packing warehouses; the manufacture, transportation and application of chemical fertilisers and pesticides; fertigation in hydroponic systems and automated irrigation; the refrigeration required from harvest right through the logistics chain to the point of sale (which has been shown to be cause particularly high emissions); and the production of all of the packaging required for shipping and sale. It's a worrying situation and information about the impact of the floriculture industry on the environment is not widely available.

Interestingly, recent research into carbon emissions has shown that flowers grown in heated glasshouses in Europe have a higher carbon footprint than flowers grown and exported from Africa. This demonstrates that calculating carbon footprint is complex and the energy required to grow out-of-season flowers in a heated glasshouse is potentially more damaging than flowers grown and flown to Europe from farms near the equator. But sustainability isn't just about carbon footprint – we also need to think about people and profit.

Opposite *Ranunculus* 'Amandine Salmon' and *Tulipa* 'Aveyron' and 'Salmon Jimmy'

While a lot of work has been done by the industry to improve conditions on flower farms, there is a long way to go in terms of addressing the issues farm workers face. One example is the excessive chemical use in flower production, which has led to negative impacts on farm employees, local biodiversity, groundwater (through contamination) and potential chemical residue risks to florists. Workers should have rights of access to medical services, while social justice matters, such as land ownership and use, fair wages, labour rights, child labour and gender issues in the workplace all require attention. There are questions about water use on farms in areas of the world where water is scarce – a lot of water is required for the production of cut flowers. Waste is another huge issue for the floristry industry, particularly the use of single-use plastics, microplastics and floral foam. We can see that for the most part the global floriculture industry doesn't operate in a way that ensures a sustainable future for all of us. So what's the alternative?

The 'slow flowers' movement is the antithesis of the fast, immediate and unsustainable global trade in cut flowers. The ethos is similar to that of the slow food movement, which encourages us to think about how our consumption impacts on people and the planet; slow food embraces the connection between the food on our plates and the food producers. It aims to promote the protection of the natural environment while rejecting unsustainable food production processes. In the same way, the slow flowers movement aims to make closer connections between flower buyers and flower farmers, focusing on provenance and supporting seasonal, locally grown flowers that are farmed in a sustainable or regenerative way. The movement wants people to reconnect with the pleasure of using seasonally available blooms and to value growing processes that put the welfare of people and the planet first.

GROW WITH THE SEASONS

Floral arranging is an art in which all of the elements of colour, movement, rhythm and light come into play through the medium of flowers. When you grow your own cut flowers, something different comes into flower each week through the growing season. Every week is an opportunity to celebrate the changing nature of our gardens and to explore the diverse range of plant material that we are able to grow. The UK has a long record of plant hunting, breeding and research as a result of its imperialist history; this means that today, our gardens are filled with plant species from across the world which have greatly enriched our outdoor spaces. There is a convenience to conventional floristry practice that means that you design first and then

You'll notice that there is something that feels just right when you have varieties that would naturally flower at the same time of year arranged together in a floral display. Spring beauties such as tulips sit comfortably among fellow spring flowers like narcissi and fritillaries, but can seem a little incongruous when arranged with summer's roses, agapanthus or veronica. Working with seasonal floral material will lend your arrangements a real sense of the garden, bringing the outdoors inside in the truest sense. It's a joyful experience to gather and arrange a vase of blooms that reflects the essence of your seasonal garden; a moment of the year captured in flowers.

Growing with the seasons can result in naturally harmonious floral arrangements such as this spring vase, which includes ranunculus, *Hesperis matronalis* (sweet rocket), allium and camassia

purchase the flowers you require to create your arrangement. Working solely with seasonal flowers can present a particular challenge (and disruption) to your creativity – it's a very different proposition to work solely with floral material gathered at the peak of perfection in that moment, rather than buying in specific varieties of flowers to carry out a design recipe.

What makes a good cut flower?

We are so lucky to have thousands of varieties of flowers to grow in our gardens, with seed catalogues and plant nurseries offering many tempting choices. With so much floral material to choose from, how do you decide what to grow and which varieties to combine in order to create your seasonal arrangements throughout the year? This chapter will help you to decide what makes a good cut flower for you.

HYDRATION

Not all plants that are grown in our gardens are suitable for cutting. Some simply don't hydrate well once cut, which means that they are completely unsuitable for the vase. Varieties of pear once in full leaf, for instance, don't take up water easily and the leaves wilt horribly. *Hyacinthus non-scripta* (English bluebell) plucked from the garden (*never* from wild spaces) will only last a day, as they are also difficult to keep hydrated, while *Hyacinthoides hispanica* (Spanish bluebell) will last a week in the vase and fill a room with a honeyed scent in mid-spring. Understanding which specific plants and cultivars hydrate well and are good for cutting is the key to the success of your cutting garden.

Species that do not make good cut flowers:

PYRUS (PEAR) The flowers shatter (drop) quickly, it has an unpleasant scent and is difficult to hydrate.

SALIX (WILLOW) The catkins on bare stems in winter work well and are beautiful, but in full leaf in summer, stems will not hydrate.

SAMBUCUS (ELDER) This is difficult to hydrate and has no vase life, while the fruits split and stain surfaces easily.

VASE LIFE

Vase life is a key factor to consider (see page 132). Some flowers, such as chrysanthemums, may have a vase life of between seven and 14 days, and give you well over a week if looked after carefully. If longevity is your priority, then careful research will tell you all you need to know about the varieties that will fulfil this requirement, and there are many flowers that will last at least a week once they've been cut and conditioned properly (see page 128). Some flowers have a fleeting vase life, but this doesn't necessarily mean they are less suitable for cutting, particularly if you are growing them for your own enjoyment. The pleasure that the heady scent of a garden rose brings for a couple of days is worth every short moment, and the graceful fall of the petals is all part of its joy. In fact, scent is quite often a defining factor in vase life; it is intrinsically linked to the senescence of flowers (the process by which a bloom matures, fades and dies). The stronger the scent, the shorter the vase life is likely to be. This is why many flowers that are purchased from shops have no perfume – the scent has been bred out of certain cultivars in order to extend the vase life, particularly those stems that are shipped for sale across the world. Growing highly scented blooms in the garden allows us to enjoy every element of the cut-flower experience, even if only for a short time.

Some flowers don't hold on to their petals once cut, and although the stems hydrate well, the petals fall after a couple of days in a process called 'shattering'. Branches of spring blossom are particularly prone to this, as is *Lunaria annua* (honesty) when it is in flower in spring – this is best grown for its seedheads rather than as a fresh cut flower. It is lovely to enjoy the fleeting beauty of certain varieties as long as you don't mind clearing up the mess they leave in their wake.

STEM LENGTH

The length of a flower's stem plays a part in any arrangement. A decent stem length means that your floral material is more versatile and you will be able to create all manner of arrangements with it. A minimum length of 45cm (18in) is preferable

Opposite Tulips and ranunculus with long stem lengths **Above** Spring blooms including alliums

arrange with. Straighter stems are easy to use, although the occasional kink or twist can create a sense of movement and enliven your floral design.

SCENT

Scent is that elusive element that transforms an arrangement into something special. It is scent that triggers a memory or an association for me, as for many others. As this is a quality that is often missing from flowers that are bought in shops, I always recommend growing as many scented flowers as you can to fill your home with floral perfume. Just one stem of flowering jasmine tucked into an arrangement will fill a room with its fragrance.

LOVE

What flowers do you actually love? Which varieties make your heart sing? Whatever they are, check that they are a useful flower for cutting, and then make them the focus of your cut flower garden. Don't grow plants you don't like just because they may fit some arbitrary floristry rules – you'll never end up using them in arrangements. Think about the varieties, colours, shapes and scents that delight you, then fill your home with flowers that you have grown with love. The wonderful thing is that we all love different things and there is a favourite flower out there for everyone.

for making up bouquets and longer stems will be necessary for larger arrangements. When buying, check the final heights of your plant selections, and try to avoid anything listed as a compact variety as these will usually produce stems that are too short to be useful in lots of contexts. Short stems have limited uses, but can be delightful when arranged in bud vases. Pruning woody shrubs at the right time of year can help to produce excellent long stems for floristry work.

GROWTH HABIT

Growth habit is equally important: a tangled mass of stems can produce some unusual and interesting shapes, but these may be quite difficult to

Growing plants for floral design

When deciding which plants you would like to grow for the vase, you need to consider that you are growing for a purpose. A good starting point is to think about the various forms of the floral material that you will be using and how these can be combined to create dynamic arrangements.

There are six main types of material used for floral design: structural plants; focal and supporting flowers; filler flowers; textural material; and airy elements. Within the constraints of conventional floristry, these forms would be used to create structured, geometric arrangements abiding by strict design rules and stem counts. Recently, a more natural aesthetic has grown in popularity and this looser approach to design allows the seasonal material to lead your creativity. However, you will still need to think about the principles of balance and proportion, and how different flower forms can be used to create something pleasing to the eye.

STRUCTURE

For the most part, foliage from woody plants represents the structural element of floral design. The structure provides the leafy framework for all of your other blooms, in much the same way as trees and shrubs are used to provide structure in garden design.

The stems of shrubs and trees, sometimes in full leaf, sometimes flowering, and perhaps with coloured stems or catkins in winter, are all valuable. This structural material doesn't just have to be green or evergreen foliage – deep purple cotinus can create a sense of drama, while the changing colours of autumn foliage can set the whole tone of a floral design.

Physocarpus opulifolius 'Diabolo' (ninebark 'Diabolo') is one of my favourites for structure

The use of mixed foliage and branches in a garden-gathered arrangement are what makes a piece feel 'of the garden', and will instantly give you an indication of the season. You are unlikely to see a branch of flowering cherry blossom in a shop-bought bouquet, but a vase full of branches cut from the garden in spring is the absolute epitome of the season and will look wonderful indoors. From flowering blossom branches in spring, via philadelphus and physocarpus in summer, to the arching abelia stems in autumn, the structural elements are your first link to the time of year and will be instrumental in defining the shape and flow of your arrangement.

Using interesting foliage such as eucalyptus, elaeagnus and physocarpus can support and enhance the flowers in your arrangements

FOCAL AND SUPPORTING FLOWERS

Focal flowers are the showstoppers of your arrangements. Taking inspiration from the principles of garden design, the focal point in a garden is used to draw and rest the eye, and this is exactly the same for floral arranging.

Focals tend to be large, blowsy blooms that instantly catch your attention: think double tulips and ranunculus in spring; peonies, roses and sunflowers in summer; and chrysanthemums and dahlias in autumn. These focals are often rounded in shape and the colour choice can determine the colour scheme for a design. Typically you will need a smaller proportion of focal flowers than fillers and foliage

Varieties of ranunculus (such as this striking 'Amandine Pink Picotee') make perfect spring focal flowers

for an arrangement (unless you are creating an opulent, luxurious display); just a few of these blooms can make a big impact.

Supporting flowers in your arrangements can be broken down into different groups by shape. They are used as a contrast to your focal bloom. Spikes and spires will include varieties such as delphiniums, foxgloves and antirrhinum – their linear form creates a vertical accent, adding height, drama and dynamism to your floral arrangement. Disc-shaped flower heads such as ammi, echinacea and daucus add another layer of interest. When using supporting flowers, consider their size and shape in relation to the focals and how the colour supports and enhances them.

Delicate grasses such as *Avena sativa* (oat) and *Briza maxima* (greater quaking grass) add another dimension of light and texture

FILLERS, TEXTURE AND AIRY ELEMENTS

Filler flowers are essential to bulking out a display, filling the space between the larger blooms and knitting the design together. This type of material will often have smaller flowers and branching heads like autumn-flowering asters or the perennial rudbeckia 'Henry Eilers'. Some fillers can be used to provide another shade of green to enhance that sense of the garden: alchemilla, bupleurum, cerinthe and mint fit into this category. Using a mixture of filler material can help to develop a colour scheme and add scent to arrangements.

Filler flowers such as *Alchemilla mollis* (lady's mantle) and salvias bridge the space between focals and add another layer of interest

In a shift away from traditional floristry dominated by hybrid tea roses, chrysanthemums and carnations, the addition of textural elements will completely change the aesthetic of your floral arranging. Our gardens are filled with buds, seedheads and grasses throughout the year, and you can make use of this material to add texture, light and rhythm to your displays. Poppy seedheads together with roses in early summer or sparkling grasses with dahlias in autumn can give a more natural, garden-like sensibility to a design and nod to the abundance of each season you are gathering the flowers in.

The joy of using such a wide range of plants for cutting is that there are unusual varieties you can use from the garden that you wouldn't typically be able to find in a traditional florist's shop. Airy elements are those dancing blooms on long thin stems that add movement and that final bit of magic to an arrangement. Aquilegia float like butterflies with their long-spurred flowers in late spring, delicate panicles of *Stipa gigantea* (golden oats) look like drops of shimmering gold come midsummer, and sanguisorba can add a pop of lightness when paired with dahlias in late summer. Playful, whimsical and wild!

Above Using a mix of flower shapes will create dynamic arrangements with layers of texture and interest
Opposite A monochrome palette and interesting flower shapes combine in this group, which includes *Anemone × hybrida* (Japanese anenome), *Digitalis purpurea* 'Bondana' (foxglove 'Bondana'), scabious and *Gladiolus murielae* (Abyssinian gladiolus)

How much to grow

As a general rule you should consider dividing your space so that you are planting one third focal flowers to two thirds fillers and foliage. When you are selecting which varieties to plant it's useful to refer back to the flower type to make sure you have enough of each of the shapes for your arrangements. Make sure at this stage that you also have plentiful supplies of each colour for every season – a simple spreadsheet can help you to plan your planting efficiently.

It's a useful exercise to take notes and build up a recipe book of arrangement ingredients throughout the year, making a note of varieties that flower at the same time and colours and shapes that work well together. This will be an invaluable tool for planning your planting in future years. Here are some ideas to get you started.

MID-SPRING MAUVE AND WHITE
STRUCTURE *Eucalyptus gunnii* (cider gum)
FOCALS *Ranunculus* 'Amandine Purple Jean' and 'Amandine White' (Persian buttercup)
SUPPORTING *Tulipa* 'Mount Tacoma' (tulip)
FILLER *Anemone* 'Galilee Pastel Mixed' (garden anemone)
TEXTURE *Cytisus × praecox* 'Albus' (broom)
AIRY *Fritillaria uva-vulpis* (fox's grape fritillary)

EARLY JUNE PASTELS
STRUCTURE *Physocarpus* (ninebark)
FOCAL *Paeonia* (peony)
SUPPORTING *Digitalis* (foxglove)
FILLER *Agrostemma githago* (corncockle)
TEXTURE *Astrantia* (masterwort)
AIRY *Silene* (campion)

EARLY AUTUMN JEWEL TONES
STRUCTURE *Abelia* (abelia)
FOCAL *Dahlia* (dahlia)
SUPPORTING *Antirrhinum* (snapdragon)
FILLER *Symphyotrichum* (Michaelmas daisy)
TEXTURE *Daucus* (wild carrot)
AIRY *Panicum* (switch grass)

Opposite Spring-flowering *Ranunculus* 'Amandine Salmon' and 'Amandine Chamallow'

Choosing colours

Colour elicits an emotional response from us and we each respond to it in a different way. The visual nature of floral material means that the colour scheme is one of the first things we notice, whether it's a bouquet in the hand or an image on social media. As a garden designer I always consider a planting scheme in terms of a colour palette, developing thoughtful combinations with the wealth of material I have to work with. I look at cut flowers in much the same way, thinking carefully about how I want to combine colours in the vase and how a particular hue can enhance the effect of the arrangement. When you are growing your own, there is always a new colour combination to discover and delight in.

PASTEL OR BRIGHT

Let's first think in terms of a general palette – do you love bright or pastel colours? You need to think about how all of your plant choices will work together in an arrangement, and you want to be able to use everything that you growing. If you have a selection of lovely pastel pinks and mauves, think

about a range of additional colours that can be used to blend or create an accent within that scheme – deeper rose pinks and cream for instance. A bright pop of canary yellow is going to be difficult to incorporate with soft shell pink, so if you love bright shades, select varieties with deeply saturated hues that work well together. If you love a colour clash, then just go for a little bit of everything to create an eclectic palette that defies all of the rules.

WARM OR COOL

Colours can appear on either the warm or cool side of the spectrum, depending on how much a primary hue leans towards either a blue or yellow bias. So red isn't just plain red: a deep magenta has a cool blue undertone whereas the red of *Geum* 'Mrs J. Bradshaw' has a warm yellow undertone. Think about whether your palette of flowers sits on the warm or cool side of the spectrum, as this will affect how your flowers appear together in the vase. This also applies to the foliage that you choose to use: deep, grey-blue greens and silver tones are cool, while fresh, limey greens are warm. These don't necessarily sit well when combined together, so consider the colour temperature of the foliage and textural elements, too.

Opposite A late spring bunch with garden anemones, ranunculus, *Geum* 'Totally Tangerine', alliums, *Hesperis matronalis* var. *albiflora* (white sweet rocket), *Silene latifolia* (white campion), camassia and nepeta

BRIDGING

As you learn to grow and arrange flowers you'll find that some are not a single block of colour, but in fact have a mix of colours within the petals. These blooms are particularly useful in floristry as they can be used to tie different elements of a design together. They incorporate the separate colours of other floral material used in an arrangement and provide the colour link that brings all disparate elements together in a cohesive design.

For example, *Helianthus* 'Ruby Eclipse' has beautiful buff-yellow petals flushed through with red and it's the perfect bridge between burgundy red sanguisorba and scabious, and pale, creamy-yellow *Gladiolus* 'Halley', as they all flower together in late summer. 'Halley' also has a red stripe on its fall petal, while nigella seedheads are green flushed through with red, and can further support the colour scheme.

Ranunculus 'Friandine White Picotee' looks like the edges of the petals have been dipped in purple ink and it's the perfect bridging flower for soft, creamy double tulips and narcissi, together with mauve-purple fritillaries and the wine-red *Anemone coronaria* 'Bordeaux'.

ACCENT AND CONTRAST

It's always pleasing to the eye to see a blend of colours artfully arranged, and the use of an accent colour can lift and change the feel of an

Tulips come in almost every hue, so plant a selection for use in both pastel and bright arrangements

as important a part in accenting the colour of your flowers.

Another type of accent colour is a contrasting hue, determined by looking at what is on the opposite side of the colour wheel. One popular colour scheme is a blend of cream and peach with a pop of pale baby blue – as long as the blue isn't too dark and sits alongside the other colours tonally, it works beautifully. Similarly, a mix of mauve and purple with a pop of orange can be an energising colour scheme – it's all about finding those shades that work well in contrast and enhance each other when arranged together.

MONOCHROMATIC SCHEMES

While some people love a mix of colours, others lean towards schemes that use just one hue. If you are a lover of just one colour and would prefer to grow a very refined palette of flowers, then you have to consider your plant choices thoughtfully. The White Garden at Sissinghurst in East Sussex has always been an inspiration to me and is the perfect example of a single-colour planting scheme. There you'll find all white flowers, but lots of layers of seasonal interest in the different flower shapes and green textural foliage throughout the year. Think about how you can bring depth and interest to an arrangement by layering various shapes and textures of flowers within your restricted colour palette.

Soft shades of apricot and salmon blend to create a pleasing tonal display of roses

arrangement completely. Looking at the colour flushing through the petals of a rose you may discover a deeper tone – taking that as inspiration you can add blooms in this 'accent' colour to provide further depth and interest.

Remember to consider foliage colour, too. There's the deep burgundy of heuchera or cotinus leaves, as well as the coppery leaves of beech trees in the autumn; foliage can play just

33

Growing flowers for dried designs

One of the most carbon-friendly ways of enjoying flowers through the winter season is to dry blooms from the garden that have been picked at the height of summer just for this purpose. A wide range of varieties can be used to create long-lasting arrangements if they are carefully cut and dried during the growing season to retain their natural colours and textures. Consider what and how much to grow as part of your annual plan: some plants make better dried material than others, and if you want to use some in fresh as well as dried displays, you will need to grow a greater quantity (see page 135 for more drying flowers).

The trend for everlasting flowers has grown considerably in recent years, but it cannot be assumed that just because something originally came from a plant that it is 'natural'. Flowers grown and cut for drying on an industrial scale often come with a greater chemical load and carbon footprint than fresh flowers: as well as the chemical cocktail used in the drying process, stems may have also been dyed, bleached or sprayed with paint or glitter. These altered stems are also often plasticised in order to preserve them indefinitely, and present yet another waste disposal problem in the form

Grasses such as setaria and pennisetum can be included in your planting plan

of microplastic contamination. They shouldn't be composted or disposed of in a way that may cause further environmental damage, which makes the case for growing your own even more compelling.

02

Plan
Shape the space and select the right plants

Planning your space

Once you've decided to grow your own cut flowers, you need to think about where you're going to grow them. Will you be growing plants for cutting within your existing borders or do you have enough room to set up a dedicated cutting garden? Will you be planting directly in the ground or will your flowers be in containers and raised beds? Is the area in sun or shade? Start by making an assessment of your site to ascertain what space and conditions you are working with and what you need to do to ready it for planting.

If you only want to cut a few blooms each week, it is practical (and lovely) to be able to snip a few flowers from the existing borders in your garden. If you have the space, a dedicated cutting garden, much like a vegetable patch, will provide the perfect workspace for growing more flowers. Bear in mind that a cutting garden is intended to be a productive growing area rather than a space designed to look good all year round. You will often be cutting plants before the flowers open in order to prolong vase life, and also stripping them out and replanting with new crops to maximise your harvest through the seasons. In this sort of situation it can be useful to think of your plants as a crop and understand that they are not there to ornament the garden.

A PLANNING CHECKLIST

It's important to consider how you want to lay out and manage your plot before you get started. Put your ideas down on paper and work out your spacings properly before ever picking up a spade. A clear plan will help you to make the best use of the space you have. If you have a budget, allocate spending appropriately once all of the elements of your cutting garden have been accounted for. To help you get started on your plan, here are some helpful things to think about.

CHECK THE ASPECT A south- or west-facing plot is ideal as it will get plenty of sunlight through the day, which will allow you to grow the widest range range of plants. A north- or east-facing plot is usually cooler and shadier, meaning that you will need to look for varieties of cut flowers that favour these conditions, such as hydrangeas, astilbes and ferns. It is advisable to lay out your beds in a north-south orientation in order to maximise the amount of light reaching your plants for optimum growth (see diagram on page 40).

ASSESS THE SPACE Start by measuring the plot: you will need to know the overall length and width of your growing area to formulate a layout plan.

Remember to leave adequate space for access – if you are planning a sizable cutting garden, you'll need pathways wide enough for a wheelbarrow to pass through. Potentially you will also need space for compost bays, a propagation area or greenhouse, as well as somewhere to store tools, so bear this in mind and work out how you can fit the maximum amount of productive space within the growing area.

DEVISE A PLAN This will be an ongoing process as you select the plants you want to grow, but it is useful to organise the space around the different plant types that you are growing. For example, if you have a

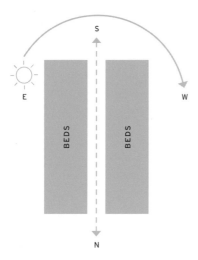

A north-south orientation
Beds set out this way will get the sun from the east in the morning, the south at midday and the west from afternoon to early evening

plot dedicated to cut flowers, it's good to have specific beds for perennial plants, which will remain in the same space for a number of years, as well as separate, dedicated beds for annuals and biennials which are grown and cut within one or two seasons. Annuals and bulbs can be easily interplanted with perennials in a mixed border to add to the variety of each season.

RESEARCH AND PURCHASE CONTAINERS If you have limited space and plan to grow in containers, think about what type would give you sufficient space for the plants you want to grow, and how many containers can be arranged in the space available to maximise access to light and make picking easy (see page 44 for more on small gardens). If you are growing in containers, use a peat-free growing medium that's suitable for the varieties you are planning to sow or plant. Pots are also a great solution if the plant you have your heart set on isn't compatible with your soil type.

ESTABLISH THE SOIL TYPE
A simple test can show whether you have clay, loam or sandy soil. Take a sample from one of your growing beds – take soil from a depth of 10-20cm (4–8in) – and moisten it with water. Can you mould the sample into a ball that holds its shape? A clay soil will hold together in a ball and feel smooth on the surface when rubbed. Loam

They are very free draining, and also leach away nutrients. They do warm up quickly in spring, which is good for direct sowing.

DO A SOIL TEST Remember that you are going to be growing fairly intensively to produce a number of crops through the seasons. The basis of good husbandry is to feed the soil, which in turn ensures that you are able to grow healthy, robust plants. A simple home soil test can be bought online or at a garden centre and can determine the balance of nitrogen, phosphorus and potassium levels in the soil, which are essential for healthy plant growth. A mulch of organic matter applied once a year should improve your soil structure and deliver a good supply of nutrients to sustain most plant growth.

The pH level of the soil relates to its acidity/alkalinity, and the ideal soil pH will sit somewhere between pH6.5 and pH7.0. Soils registering below pH6.5 are acidic, while anything above pH7.5 is alkaline. Amendments can be made to adjust the pH, but I recommend growing plants that suit your soil.

may form a ball but it won't hold its shape as well as clay, while a sandy soil will feel gritty and crumble when rolled.

Clay soils are formed of the smallest soil particles. They hold on to moisture and nutrients well, but the surface can dry out and crack in hot weather. Loam soils are a good balance of large and small soil particles and are moisture retentive yet free draining; they provide an ideal soil type for a wide range of plants. Sandy soils are formed of relatively large particles.

CONSIDER ACCESS TO WATER
Water is essential for healthy plant growth, particularly for cut flowers where consistent watering at the right time in the plant life-cycle is essential for increasing the stem length. If you

have a large area for growing you may want to consider an irrigation system which can save a huge amount of time watering plants and is also a very resource-efficient way to keep your plants hydrated. A drip irrigation system is highly effective and reduces water usage by applying it directly to the soil above the roots, exactly where it is needed. Overhead watering with a sprinkler can damage flowers and cause fungal problems once they are in bloom.

Look at where it may be possible to install water butts to collect rainwater from roofs, or think about harvesting grey water from the house for use in garden beds. Grey water from the bathroom sink, bathtub or shower (not the kitchen sink) can be siphoned off and stored in butts. Remember that you will also require easy access to clean, fresh water for washing and filling buckets for cutting flowers.

IS THE AREA SHELTERED OR EXPOSED? Wind can be a limiting factor when growing flowers and can cause a lot of damage on exposed sites, even when plant supports are used. Do you have space to plant a natural windbreak? Shrubs or tall grasses such as miscanthus can be used to create windbreaks and double up as material for cutting too. Alternatively, you can install netting to slow wind speeds and prevent plant damage.

Mint for foliage, including *Mentha suaveolens* (apple mint), back right; *M. longifolia* Buddleia Mint Group (back left); and *M. × piperita* f. *citrata* 'Chocolate' (chocolate peppermint) in the front

CHOOSE A METHOD OF WEED CONTROL While weeds are an essential part of the garden habitat for insects, your cutting garden will function more efficiently if you can minimise weed growth within your beds. Weeds will compete with your plants for water and nutrients, and their fast growth can quickly crowd out flower seedlings. Fluff from seedheads can stick to the leaves and petals of your cut stems, which is not ideal, and of course you do not want thousands more weed seeds germinating in your productive growing space.

In a small or container garden, a little bit of hand-weeding or hoeing may be sufficient to keep on top of any weeds. In a larger area, weeding can take up a huge amount of time, especially at the height of summer when there are so many other jobs to do, so consider how to reduce their growth at the outset.

Keeping the soil covered is an effective way to stay on top of weed growth – this works by excluding light from reaching the soil surface which prevents weed seeds from germinating. Either use a deep mulch of compost, bark or straw (not hay, which is full of seed!) or plant through landscape fabric, burning holes at set spacings. Although landscape fabric is a plastic product, it can be reused for many years, which means its carbon footprint can be lower than that of commercially produced compost which has to be brought in every season.

BE PART OF THE ECOSYSTEM Our gardens are part of a wider ecosystem and our cultivated plants often provide a gourmet buffet for wildlife. The garden wildlife will vary depending on your location and you may find that a number of animals enjoy the fruits of your labour more than you do. Rabbits, deer, foxes, voles, pigeons, mice, slugs and many more creatures will eat your bulbs and corms, new shoots and flower buds, so assess the situation and think about what protection you may need for your plants in the new growing space.

While many animals can wreak havoc in the garden, a friend once shared a quote with me, which I love: 'If something isn't eating your plants, then your garden is not part of the ecosystem.' We very much want to work with nature rather than against it, but it can be dispiriting if the squirrels dig up *all* of your tulip bulbs. In some places a little bit of protective netting may make the difference between having some flowers to harvest or just growing expensive snacks.

ASSIGN A SPACE FOR PROCESSING
Do you have a place where you can process your blooms once they've been cut? Stripping leaves when preparing stems for conditioning can create a lot of mess, which you may not want to have in the house, particularly if you have a large garden producing many stems each week. A small space in a shed is ideal. A dark, cool place where the flowers can rest to rehydrate once cut will also be required – a bathroom, cupboard under the stairs or a garage can be used if you don't have a separate workspace.

Difficult spaces

SMALL GARDENS

It's so important to plan carefully for a small garden in order to maximise your production. Where containers are used for growing, aim for the largest possible rather than many small pots. You want the plants to have room for a good root system, particularly for cut-and-come-again varieties, to ensure they are productive for as long as possible. Think about growing vertically – climbers can churn out flowers for months and take up little floor space.

If you only have room for one pot, try the following combination for flowers for most of the year. Start by sowing sweet peas in autumn which will bloom for you in early summer. These could be underplanted with spring-flowering bulbs for an early-season crop. You should be able to cut from the sweet peas for a couple of months in early summer before they run out of steam. Once over, remove them from the container, refresh the compost and replant with a pot-grown dahlia or annual rudbeckia, which will give you flowers until the first frosts.

SHADY GARDENS

There is no doubt that it is much more difficult to grow annual varieties of cut flowers in a shady space, but there are a number of bulbs, herbaceous perennials and shrubs that can provide a wealth of material. Ferns are fantastic in low light areas and look wonderful in arrangements. There are also many roses that perform well in partial shade. From spring to autumn it is possible to have something in flower for the vase. Here are some other seasonal ideas:

Spring *Anemone coronaria* (garden anemone), *Aquilegia* (columbine), *Hyacinthoides hispanica* (Spanish bluebell), *Euphorbia* (spurge), *Fritillaria* (fritillary), *Helleborus* (hellebore), *Lamprocapnos spectabilis* (bleeding heart), *Narcissus* (daffodil), *Tellima grandiflora* (fringe cups)

Summer *Alchemilla* (lady's mantle), *Amsonia* (bluestar), *Astilbe* (astilbe), *Astrantia* (masterwort), *Campanula persicifolia* (peach-leaved bellflower), *Digitalis* (foxglove), *Gillenia* (Bowman's root), *Heuchera* (heuchera),

Autumn *Anemone × hybrida* 'Honorine Jobert' (Japanese anemone), *Euonymus europaeus* (spindle), *Hydrangea* (hydrangea), *Symphyotrichum* (Michaelmas daisy)

Winter *Corylus* (hazel), *Garrya elliptica* (silk tassel bush), *Nandina* (heavenly bamboo), *Sarcococca confusa* (sweet box), *Skimmia* (skimmia), *Viburnum tinus* (laurustinus)

Selecting plants

Once your garden infrastructure is sorted it's time to think about plants. To provide flowers for cutting right through the growing season, plan to grow a mix of plant types, including annuals, biennials, herbaceous perennials, trees, shrubs, climbers and bulbs.

ANNUALS

This group of plants will provide masses of colour and variety for your cutting garden through the year. Annuals need to be sown every year, and they grow, flower, set seed and die all within one growing season. There are two different types of annual plants: hardy and half hardy.

Hardy annuals These are frost tolerant and can be sown in late summer/early autumn for the earliest crop of annuals the following year. However, these are often sown both under cover and directly outdoors fairly early in the year from late winter into spring. They can also be sown in succession through spring to provide flowers from early summer and into autumn.

EASY HARDY ANNUALS

- *Ammi* (ammi)
- *Centaurea cyanus* (cornflower)
- *Cerinthe* (honeywort)
- *Daucus carota* (wild carrot)
- *Delphinium consolida* (larkspur)

- *Lavatera trimestris* (royal mallow)
- *Nigella* (love-in-a-mist)
- *Scabiosa* (scabious)
- *Tanacetum parthenium* (feverfew)
- *Xerochrysum bracteatum* (strawflower)

Half-hardy annuals These cannot tolerate frost or very low temperatures and must be started under cover in spring or sown outdoors once all risk of frost has passed towards the end of May. Varieties of cosmos, rudbeckia and zinnia will bloom through summer and autumn until the first frost brings their flowering to an end.

Cerinthe major (honeywort) is an easy hardy annual to grow and is beloved by bees

- *Celosia* (cock's comb)
- *Cosmos* (cosmos)
- *Helianthus annuus* (sunflower)
- *Limonium sinuatum* (statice)
- *Nicotiana* (tobacco plant)
- *Panicum elegans* (switch grass)
- *Phlox drummondii* (annual phlox)
- *Rudbeckia hirta* (coneflower)
- *Setaria* (foxtail millet)
- *Zinnia* (zinnia)

BIENNIALS

Biennials have a two-season life-cycle which must include a period of vernalisation to produce a crop. This means that they must be exposed to low winter temperatures to induce flowering stems; in mild winters, warm temperatures mean poor flower production for this group of plants.

Ideally seed should be sown between May and June (before midsummer) and young plants need to be transplanted to their final growing positions by mid- to late-summer to give them plenty of time to produce a well-developed root system before the winter weather sets in. They will continue to grow slowly through winter, and as spring temperatures start to rise, they will finally come into flower in May and June. I grow some annuals as biennials for a longer growing season and for better quality flowers.

Biennials are a particularly useful group that give a crop during the 'May gap' – the lean period between the late spring bulbs coming to an end and the early summer crops starting to flower.

EASY BIENNIALS (OR TREAT AS BIENNIALS)

- *Agrostemma githago* (corncockle)
- *Anchusa* (bugloss)
- *Campanula medium* (Canterbury bells)
- *Dianthus barbatus* (sweet William)
- *Digitalis* (foxglove)
- *Lunaria* (honesty)
- *Erysimum* (wallflower)
- *Hesperis* (sweet rocket)
- *Orlaya* (laceflower)
- *Papaver nudicaule* (Icelandic poppy)

PERENNIALS

Herbaceous and woody perennials are the backbone of the cutting garden. They live for a number of years and therefore require a permanent planting position on your plot. Because they flower at the same time each year they reflect the true seasonality of the garden in the vase, as opposed to some annuals which can be sown at different times of the year to produce a harvest.

Perennials are easily purchased as small plants, plugs or as bare-root plants in winter. Young perennial plants can be planted at any time, as long as the soil is not frozen, but autumn and spring are usually best for planting out. They grow quickly once planted and will start to give

require a period of cold in order to trigger germination; either place seed in the freezer for a few weeks before sowing, or leave a tray sown with seed outside through winter and they will germinate the following spring.

As a general rule, perennials are much less labour-intensive to grow than annuals, and will perform consistently in the cutting garden during those periods of intemperate weather that can adversely affect annuals. However, perennials can also be hardy or half-hardy: anything labelled as half-hardy may not tolerate very low winter temperatures or frost, and must be treated as an annual or brought in under cover during winter.

Herbaceous perennials The top growth of most herbaceous perennials dies back to ground level completely over winter and produces new leaves and flowering shoots each spring.

Grow a sunflower like 'Valentine' in succession to cut through the summer and autumn months

There is a huge range of cutting varieties to choose from to suit every situation, whether you grow in a dry, sandy garden or a cool garden on heavy, clay soil. Some plants, such as peonies, will have a very short cutting window of perhaps seven to ten days in the whole year, while others – mint is one good example – will keep producing stems from late spring to late summer. Search out particular named varieties of perennials that have exceptional qualities for cutting.

you a decent crop of stems within a couple of years.

Most perennials can be grown from seed, while some special cultivars can only be propagated vegetatively and must be bought as plants. Most perennial seed will germinate readily if it is fresh, and for this reason I like to gather seed when it is ripe on the plant and sow it right away – this is usually in late summer and autumn. Some seeds

The ephemeral beauty of early cherry blossom is a delight in the vase

Woody perennials Floristry stems that come from shrubs and trees are often referred to as 'woodies' by cut flower growers. Woody perennials either have a single stem (trees) or multiple stems (shrubs) that emerge from ground level, and they can be either deciduous or evergreen. Both trees and shrubs provide a wealth of cutting material throughout the year.

Pruning at specific times of the year will help to produce long, straight stems for flower arranging, rather than a woody thicket that is difficult to use in a vase. You need to know whether the plant you have produces flowers on the current year's wood or the previous year's wood – this tells you how and when to prune to ensure you get flowers. As a general rule, woodies that flower on the current year's stems should be pruned down to a bud in winter or early spring, whereas a plant that flowers on the previous year's wood should be pruned immediately after flowering to generate new growth for flowering the following year.

EASY HERBACEOUS PERENNIALS

- *Achillea* (yarrow)
- *Agapanthus* (African lily)
- *Alchemilla* (lady's mantle)
- *Astrantia* (masterwort)
- *Delphinium* (delphinium)
- *Eryngium* (sea holly)
- *Geum* (avens)
- *Mentha* (mint)
- *Paeonia* (peony)
- *Sedum* (stonecrop)

EASY WOODY PERENNIALS

- *Abelia* (abelia)
- *Brachyglottis* (senecio)
- *Cytisus* (broom)
- *Eucalyptus* (gum)
- *Physocarpus* (ninebark)
- *Pittosporum* (pittosporum)
- *Rosa* (rose)
- *Salix* (willow)
- *Syringa* (lilac)
- *Viburnum* (viburnum)

BULBS, CORMS AND TUBERS

Certain plants have modified stems in the form of bulbs, corms and tubers. This group of plants offers a wide range of variety for cutting. Some of these are annual and need to be planted every year, while others are reliably perennial and can also be lifted and divided to increase your plant stocks. Many spring flowers grow from bulbs and corms, and they are an essential component of the garden. Each variety has a specific planting time and will need to be planted either in autumn for spring flowers, or in spring for summer- and autumn-flowering blooms.

Narcissi are one of the earliest spring bulbs

EASY BULBS/CORMS/TUBERS

- *Allium* (allium)
- *Anemone coronaria* (garden anemone)
- *Dahlia* (dahlia)
- *Fritillaria* (fritillary)
- *Gladiolus* (sword lily)
- *Gladiolus murielae* (Abyssinian gladiolus)
- *Narcissus* (daffodil)
- *Nerine* (nerine)
- *Ranunculus* (Persian buttercup)
- *Tulipa* (tulip)

CLIMBING PLANTS

These have long stems that twine around or cling to supports. They are either scandent or trailing and provide another interesting element to floral arrangements. Care needs to be taken with their supports and when cutting so as not to damage fragile stems. Perennial climbers can be purchased and planted from autumn to spring. Sweet peas are hardy annuals and can be sown in autumn for an early summer crop or in succession in spring for flowers later in the season. Most other annual climbers can be sown in spring.

EASY CLIMBERS

- *Akebia quinata* (chocolate vine)
- *Clematis* (clematis)
- *Cobaea scandens* (cup-and-saucer vine)
- *Humulus lupulus* (hop)
- *Jasminum* (jasmine)
- *Lathyrus* (sweet pea)
- *Lonicera* (honeysuckle)
- *Trachelospermum* (star jasmine)
- *Tropaeolum* (nasturtium)
- *Vitis vinifera* (grape vine)

Harvest and yield

When you are planning your cutting garden it is important to understand the yield and the harvest window of each variety that you would like to grow. This information will help you to plan how many plants you need, and for annuals, how often you should sow to guarantee a constant supply of flowers.

HARVEST WINDOW

Plants will fall into different harvest categories which indicates how long you will be able to cut from them. Some varieties will produce a single harvest, some will crop for about 4–6 weeks before the quality starts to decline, while others will crop consistently on a cut-and-come-again basis for weeks. Each variety has its own specific flowering time when the flowers reach peak condition for cutting – this is the harvest window.

It's easy to find out this information for perennials as they tend to flower at the same time each year, with a little variation depending on the region you are gardening in, microclimates and changes in annual weather patterns. You will find that perennial plants generally give you around 3–4 weeks of good quality material for cutting. Certain plants will only be at their peak cutting stage for ten days a year – peonies for example – but you may be able to cut plants like echinacea for ten weeks or more. One way to extend a short harvest window for perennials is to select a range of early-, mid- and late-season varieties of the same plant, which will bloom one after the other. Peonies are a great example of a perennial whose harvest window can be extended in this way. 'Coral Charm' is one of the first varieties to flower, which could be followed by pale pink 'Catharina Fontijn' and then heavily scented 'Duchesse de Nemours' – this trio will provide almost a month's worth of peonies from the garden.

Another way to extend a perennial harvest window is to use a technique called the 'Chelsea chop', which delays flowering for approximately 3–4 weeks, thereby extending the potential harvest window (see page 82).

Some annuals and perennials can be cut back after their initial harvest, and if kept well watered and fed they may produce a good secondary flush of flowers later in the season.

The harvest window can also be extended for both perennial and annual plants by covering them with a cloche or growing under cover in a greenhouse or polytunnel. A covered

Opposite *Orlaya grandiflora* (white laceflower)

growing space offers protection from the worst of the elements, as well as warmer temperatures, which bring plants into flower earlier than usual through the season – this also helps to extend flowering at the end of the year as the weather outside gets colder.

YIELD

Understanding how many stems each variety yields is also critical to making sure you grow enough plants for your needs. Yield is a variable factor when it comes to cut flower production and can be affected by soil, weather, feeding, variety selection, plant quality, frequency of watering and even the skill of the grower. There isn't a resource that will give you the yield for every variety you can grow, so you need to start making a record of your plants noting the potential of each type. For example, one plant of *Astrantia* 'Roma' can produce in excess of 100 stems in a season, whereas you may only get five stems from a ranunculus. Having some idea about yield will enable you to make decisions about how many of each to grow.

SUCCESSION SOWING

Sowing annual varieties in succession is the way to ensure a continuous supply of stems through the season. Each annual variety will fall into one of the three harvest categories: single cut, medium producer or cut-and-come-again. Once you know which category a particular variety is in, you

can work out the frequency with which you need to sow it in order to be able to cut stems for a number of weeks.

Single cut Varieties that produce a single cut from one sowing will need to be sown frequently in order to keep up enough production for a continuous supply. This means that you have to sow little and often – every 2–3 weeks – for a fresh crop of stems to cut just as the previous harvest ends.

- *Atriplex* (orache)
- *Briza* (quaking grass)
- *Bupleurum* (bupleurum)
- *Celosia* (crested) (cock's comb)
- *Helianthus* (single stem) (sunflower)
- *Matthiola* (stocks)
- *Nigella* (love-in-a-mist)
- *Phacelia tanacetifolia* (fiddleneck)
- *Setaria* (foxtail millet)

Medium producer These need to be sown just a few times through the year. They will crop for 4–6 weeks before the quality declines and the plant is ready to be removed. The varieties that fall into this category should be sown roughly every 4–6 weeks. Lots of hardy annuals are medium producers and the first succession can be sown in autumn, followed by a further two sowings in early spring and mid-spring.

- *Amaranthus* (amaranth)
- *Ammi majus* (bishop's flower)
- *Ammi visnaga* (toothpick plant)
- *Anethum graveolens* (dill)
- *Antirrhinum* (snapdragon)
- *Borago officinalis* (borage)
- *Centaurea cyanus* (cornflower)
- *Cosmos* (cosmos)
- *Cynoglossum amabile* (Chinese forget-me-not)
- *Daucus carota* (wild carrot)
- *Delphinium consolida* (larkspur)
- *Helianthus* (branching) (sunflower)
- *Lavatera trimestris* (royal mallow)
- *Lathyrus* (sweet pea)
- *Malope* (mallow wort)
- *Orlaya* (laceflower)

Cut-and-come-again These only need to be sown once, as they will continue to produce stems for cutting without a decline in quality as long as the crop is deadheaded to stop it producing seed. These crops are particularly useful in a garden with limited space as they will continue to

Nigella produces a single cut from one sowing. Its common name, love-in-a-mist, changes to devil-in-a-bush once its seedheads develop!

crop through their harvest windows with relatively little work and maximum production in a small growing area.

- *Basilicum* (basil)
- *Celosia* (feathered) (cock's comb)
- *Craspedia globosa* (drumsticks)
- *Gomphrena globosa* (globe amaranth)
- *Limonium* (statice)
- *Nicotiana* (tobacco plant)
- *Panicum* (switch grass)
- *Papaver nudicaule* (Icelandic poppy)
- *Phlox drummondii* (annual phlox)
- *Rudbeckia* (coneflower)
- *Scabiosa* (scabious)
- *Tanacetum parthenium* (feverfew)
- *Thlaspi* (pennycress)
- *Zinnia* (Zinnia)

Harvesting calendar Structure, focal and supporting flowers

	JAN	FEB	MAR	APR	MAY	JUN	JUL	AUG	SEP	OCT	NOV	DEC
Abelia							▓	▓	▓	▓		
Agapanthus							▓	▓	▓			
Allium				▓	▓	▓						
Anemone		▓	▓	▓	▓							
Anemone × hybrida								▓	▓	▓		
Antirrhinum						▓	▓	▓	▓			
Astilbe						▓	▓	▓				
Camassia				▓	▓	▓						
Campanula						▓	▓	▓				
Celosia							▓	▓				
Cytisus				▓	▓							
Dahlia							▓	▓	▓	▓		
Delphinium consolida						▓	▓	▓	▓	▓		
Digitalis					▓	▓	▓					
Echinacea							▓	▓	▓			
Eryngium							▓	▓	▓			
Eucalyptus	▓	▓	▓	▓							▓	▓
Fritillaria				▓	▓							
Gladiolus							▓	▓	▓			
Gladiolus murielae								▓	▓	▓		
Helianthus						▓	▓	▓	▓			
Helleborus			▓	▓								
Hydrangea							▓	▓	▓	▓		
Lavatera						▓	▓	▓				
Matthiola				▓	▓	▓						
Narcissus			▓	▓								
Nerine									▓	▓	▓	
Papaver nudicaule				▓	▓	▓						
Peony					▓	▓						
Phlox							▓	▓				
Physocarpus						▓	▓	▓	▓			
Pittosporum	▓	▓	▓							▓	▓	▓
Ranunculus				▓	▓	▓						
Rosa					▓	▓	▓	▓	▓			
Spiraea			▓	▓								
Syringa				▓	▓							
Tulipa			▓	▓								
Veronica						▓	▓	▓	▓			
Zinnia							▓	▓	▓	▓		

Harvesting calendar Filler, texture and airy flowers

	JAN	FEB	MAR	APR	MAY	JUN	JUL	AUG	SEP	OCT	NOV	DEC
Achillea						■	■	■	■			
Alchemilla					■	■						
Ammi						■	■	■	■			
Anethum graveolens						■	■	■	■			
Aquilegia					■	■						
Aster							■	■	■	■		
Astrantia					■	■	■	■	■			
Basilicum						■	■	■	■			
Centaurea cyanus				■	■	■						
Cerinthe					■	■	■					
Cosmos							■	■	■	■		
Crocosmia								■	■	■		
Daucus							■	■	■	■		
Dianthus barbatus					■	■	■					
Eupatorium							■	■	■			
Fritillaria			■	■								
Geum				■	■	■						
Gillenia						■	■	■				
Grasses							■	■	■	■		
Helichrysum							■	■	■			
Hesperantha									■	■		
Hesperis					■	■						
Lathyrus						■	■	■	■			
Lavandula							■	■				
Leucojum			■	■								
Linaria					■	■	■	■	■			
Lysimachia					■	■	■					
Mentha						■	■	■				
Nicotiana							■	■	■	■		
Nigella						■	■	■				
Origanum							■	■	■			
Orlaya					■	■	■					
Polemonium					■	■						
Rudbeckia								■	■	■		
Sanguisorba							■	■	■			
Scabiosa							■	■	■			
Scented-leaf pelargonium							■	■	■	■		
Silene					■	■	■					
Tanacetum parthenium						■	■	■	■			

55

Grow
Achieve an abundant harvest each season

Spring

Spring is all about the anticipation and excitement for a season filled with flowers. The dull grey of late winter is broken by the first sight of colour in the garden and from there it's a season of firsts: the scent of the first narcissus to flower, the first seeds to germinate, and the first warm day when winter jumpers are shed and you spy the first butterfly making the most of the new season. I love the pale morning light, mists and birdsong; the hum of the first bumblebee and the seedlings pushing up through the soil, heavy with the potential of the year to come.

ESSENTIAL TASKS

- Start your annual seed sowing. Don't be tempted to start sowing too early; by mid-February we have approximately ten hours of daylight, which means this is the earliest point in the year at which you should commence with sowing seeds. Seedlings started indoors in January tend to become leggy and produce poor quality plants that won't make good quality cut flowers. In early spring, start sowing hardy annual varieties, and follow these with half-hardy annual varieties in mid-spring. Make sure you check your average last frost date, as this will determine the right time to sow tender varieties, which should be sown no earlier than four weeks beforehand.

Perennials that flower in their first year can be sown in early spring for flowers later in the summer. Working to a seed-sowing plan will help to keep you organised.

- Harden off any plants grown under cover in the house, greenhouse or polytunnel by moving trays or pots outside on warm days and returning them under cover overnight. Continue to do this for a couple of weeks before you intend to plant out into beds in order to acclimatise young plants to outdoor conditions.

- Don't plant out any half-hardy annuals until after your last frost date, otherwise you risk losing them to a frosty night.

- Prepare your annual beds for direct sowing and planting any module-raised plants. Make sure that beds are free from weeds and enrich the soil with a natural fertiliser, if required. Finally, add a layer of compost, particularly if you are following the no-dig method (see page 62).

- Plant summer- and autumn-flowering bulbs such as gladioli and nerines.

- Protect new spring growth from slug and snail damage – look to natural repellents such as copper rings, wool pellets or crushed egg shells. Protect from birds with the use of netting.

- Erect supports early in the season for taller varieties.

- Divide grasses and late-flowering

The scent of the early-flowering narcissus like 'Thalia' is one of the joys of spring

perennial plants once the soil warms and they start to show signs of growth. Make sure that you water them well while they are establishing.

- Cut back spring foliage crops like eucalyptus and brachyglottis in April. The growth produced through the season will be mature enough to start cutting again for the vase in autumn.

SEED SOWING

To get started, you will need: shallow seed trays or module seed trays, peat-free seed compost, vermiculite, a garden sieve and seeds.

For tiny seeds

- Sieve the compost into a seed tray to break down any larger lumps.
- Tamp down the compost by lifting the tray and striking it smartly back down on to the table surface to knock out any air pockets and settle it in the tray.
- Cover the compost with a layer of vermiculite.
- Sow a thin layer of seed on top of the vermiculite. Lots of varieties with tiny seeds require light for germination, and the vermiculite will help to maintain the correct level of moisture and humidity around the seed, thereby improving the germination rate.
- Always remember to label the tray with the variety name and the date.
- Set the seed tray in a shallow container half filled with water; the compost will then draw up the moisture through the holes in the base of the tray. This is preferable to overhead watering which may dislodge or wash away the fine seed.
- Once the seedlings germinate, they can be pricked out (transplanted) into pots or into a module tray. Only prick them out when they have one set of true leaves (leaves that are the shape of the mature plant). Never hold seedlings by the stem; always lift the roots gently with a suitable tool (a pencil is ideal) and hold by a leaf to carefully transplant the seedling into its new container. Make sure the compost is firmed around the seedling. Water well and set aside to grow on in a sheltered area of a greenhouse, in a cold frame or on a windowsill.

For large seeds

- These can be sown into module trays to ensure there will be less root disturbance for the seedlings.
- Sieve the compost into the module tray until it is level at the top.
- Knock out the air and allow the compost to settle by striking the tray smartly on the table surface.
- Place one seed into each cell of the module tray.
- Using the sieve, cover the seeds in the tray with a layer of vermiculite.
- Label, then water from below by placing the tray in a water bath (see page 60).
- The seedlings will be ready to plant out into beds once the root system has filled the module cell and they have been hardened off in preparation for planting (see page 59).

NO-DIG BEDS

Soil is a precious resource. It is full of living things that break down organic matter to provide nutrients for plant growth – insects, fungi and microorganisms – and a healthy soil is full of life. We need to look after our soil to maintain its capacity to function as the vital ecosystem for plant growth. Digging destroys and disrupts the carefully balanced environment of the soil and its structure.

Soil is also Earth's largest store of carbon. Every time soil is turned over – dug, ploughed or tilled – carbon is released from it into the atmosphere.

Climate scientists estimate that agriculture accounts for more than ten per cent of global greenhouse gas emissions. As climate-conscious gardeners, we need to consider our growing methods and aim for them to be as sustainable as possible.

The no-dig method is one way to grow a garden sustainably. The soil is never turned over so there's very little disruption to the soil structure. This method also minimises weed growth and the negative impact on the soil's ecosystem. Even if you choose not to use this technique, it is a good idea to add organic matter to the soil annually. Remember, our aim should always be to feed the soil, not the plants. Here are some steps to creating no-dig beds.

- Cut down any weeds to ground level; they can be left on the surface as they will rot down once they are covered.
- You need some biodegradable material such as cardboard to exclude light from the soil. Lay this over the area where you wish to create the bed. Damp down with some water, and then cover the cardboard with a layer of compost that's at least 10–15cm (4–6in) deep.
- Leave the beds for six months before planting to allow time for the weeds to die and the card to rot down. Once the bed is ready you can plant seedlings or sow directly into the compost layer.
- In subsequent years, cover the bed with a 5cm (2in) layer of compost.

Spring flower harvest

Allium / **Allium** →

VARIETIES Too many lovely options to list, but I recommend 'Violet Beauty', 'Purple Sensation' (pictured) and 'Eros'. Good species include *A. hollandicum*, *A. stipitatum* and *A. nigrum*.

COLOUR Purple and mauve, plus some pink and white.

GROWING Most alliums are perennial bulbs, although some may not be reliably perennial and need to be replanted each year, depending on your growing conditions. Plant in free-draining soil in autumn for flowers from May to June. Add grit for drainage if planting into heavy soil. For small spaces, plant into pots in layers among other spring bulbs.

CUT AND CONDITION Cut when half of the flowers on the head are open.

VASE LIFE 7–10 days

DRYING Seedheads

NOTE Alliums are great for bridging the May gap, providing a focal variety for arranging in late spring. They can smell slightly onion-like when cut, but the smell will dissipate after a day or so in the vase.

Anemone coronaria / **Garden anemone**

VARIETIES Specialist cut flower varieties include 'Galilee', 'Meron', 'Jerusalem', 'Carmel', 'Mistral' and 'Full Star'.

COLOUR Pastel shades and white, plus blue, purple, burgundy and bright pink.

GROWING The corms are usually grown as an annual plant for cutting. They should be planted in autumn and grown on in beds through winter for flowers in early spring. Support netting is required to keep the stems straight, especially for crops grown outside rather than in a glasshouse or polytunnel. Consistent weekly watering is necessary for good flower production and long stems.

CUT AND CONDITION Cut when the petals have separated and the flower is starting to open. Bunch and wrap in paper and leave overnight to keep the stems straight.

VASE LIFE 7–10 days

DRYING No

NOTE The best quality flowers are produced if they are grown in a glasshouse or polytunnel where they will flower from the end of February if planted in September. Spring-planted outdoor crops will flower into June. Watch out for small rodents who like to eat the corms after they are planted.

Aquilegia vulgaris / **Columbine**

VARIETIES Other good species for cutting include *A. chrysantha* (with yellow flowers) and *A. viridiflora* (with rich purple petals under green sepals).

GROWING These are short-lived perennials which prefer partial shade and moist but free-draining soil.

CUT AND CONDITION Cut as the first flower on the stem opens and when the stamens are bright yellow.

VASE LIFE 6–7 days

DRYING Seedheads

Camassia leichtlinii 'Alba' / **Californian white-flowered quamash** ↗

GROWING Plant bulbs in autumn for flowers in April and May. Tolerant of heavier, moisture-retentive soils and pretty trouble free to grow.

CUT AND CONDITION Cut as the first few blooms begin to open up the stem; place straight into cool water.

VASE LIFE 7 days

DRYING No

← *Cerinthe major* / **Honeywort**

GROWING Sow in late summer and plant into beds in autumn for sultry purple flowers in April and May. The seed coat is hard so soak in water overnight prior to sowing. Seed can also be sown in succession in spring for flowers through the summer.

CUT AND CONDITION Cut when the first nodding flowers are fully open. The leaves and stems are fleshy, so sear for ten seconds in boiling water then plunge into buckets of cool water and

leave overnight. Wrapping the stems in paper helps them to remain straight.

VASE LIFE 7–10 days

DRYING No

Cytisus / **Broom**

VARIETIES *Cytisus × praecox* 'Albus' has arching green stems and pretty, small white flowers.

GROWING This deciduous shrub requires free-draining soil and full sun for the best flowers. It does not do well on heavier soils. Prune immediately after flowering as flowers are produced on the previous year's wood.

CUT AND CONDITION Stems can be cut in bud for the longest vase life. Otherwise cut when a third of the flowers are open along the stem and place into water.

VASE LIFE 5–7 days

DRYING No

Eucalyptus / Gum →

VARIETIES There are many species to choose from, but some that are particularly good for cut foliage include *E. gunnii* (pictured), *E. parvula*, *E. archeri*, *E. nicholii*, *E. pulverulenta* 'Baby Blue' and *E. cinerea*.

COLOUR Cool greens and silvery blues.

GROWING Eucalyptus harvesting season runs from September to March. Plants prefer well-drained soil in full sun where they are sheltered from the wind, as they can suffer from wind rock. Pollard plants in late March to produce stems with the juvenile foliage which is best for floral arranging. To do this, cut the trunk down to 90cm–1.2m (3–4ft) and prune all side shoots to within 3cm (1.25in) of the main trunk; it may look a bit drastic, but new shoots will emerge in May and these will be ready to cut in autumn. Do not let the plants dry out while they are growing through summer, as this will affect the quality of the foliage.

CUT AND CONDITION Foliage will be mature enough to cut once it hardens in September. No special conditioning required, but stems with new or immature foliage will wilt. Make sure to only cut within the harvest window.

VASE LIFE 7–10 days

DRYING It makes beautiful dried foliage which looks ethereal in wreaths.

NOTE There are many eucalyptus plants suitable for different types of growing conditions, so be sure to research which will be best for your location. Always pollard your plants, otherwise they may quickly outgrow their planting space.

Fritillaria / Fritillary

VARIETIES Small, delicate species for cutting are *F. meleagris*, *F. uva-vulpis* and *F. acmopetala*. Taller species are *F. persica* and *F. imperialis*.

COLOUR White, mauve, purple, green, black, yellow and orange.

GROWING Fritillaries are perennial bulbs that should be planted in autumn for delicate, bell-shaped flowers in spring. They prefer a moisture-retentive soil in sun and are very easy to grow with few pest or disease issues.

CUT AND CONDITION Pull rather than cut the small varieties as the stems begin to lengthen and the flowers open fully, but do this before the stamens discolour. Stems of taller varieties can be cut. Bunch and wrap all varieties in paper before placing them into water to keep the stems straight while they are conditioning.

VASE LIFE 7 days

DRYING No

NOTE *F. imperialis* can smell a bit foxy in the vase. All of the forms, whether large or small, add a sense of drama and elegance to spring displays. The sense of movement comes from the natural twist and bend of the stems.

VASE LIFE 7 days

DRYING Dry seedheads upside down.

NOTE Some varieties have upright-facing flowers and are particularly lovely in the vase as well as the garden. The tiny flowers of the nodding varieties add a pop of colour and bring a sense of graceful movement to spring arrangements. They look delicate, but are very robust cut flowers.

Gladiolus communis subsp. *byzantinus* / Byzantine gladiolus

GROWING Plant this perennial bulb in autumn in well-drained soil in full sun for late spring flowers that are a striking magenta pink.

CUT AND CONDITION Cut when the first flower begins to open; the subsequent flowers will continue to open in the vase. No special conditioning required.

VASE LIFE 7 days

DRYING No

Geum / Avens ↑

VARIETIES 'Totally Tangerine' (pictured), 'East of Eden', 'Flames of Passion' and 'Roger's Rebellion' are good varieties for cutting. Excellent species include *G. coccineum*, *G. rivale* and *G. chiloense*.

COLOUR Warm tones of orange, peach, yellow and red.

GROWING Geums are perennials that flower from late spring through to summer. They prefer a moisture-retentive soil and will thrive in sun or shade. Watch out for aphids which can be problematic early in the season.

CUT AND CONDITION Allow the petals on the first flower on the stem to drop; cut as the subsequent flowers begin to open and when the stamens are a bright rather than dull yellow. Cut early in the morning as these will not hydrate well if cut in heat; immerse immediately in deep cool water.

Helleborus / Hellebore ↗

VARIETIES *H.* × *hybridus* Ashwood Garden hybrids (pictured), and for upward-facing flowers go for cultivars of *H.* × *ballardiae* and *H.* × *ericsmithii*.

COLOUR All except orange and blue.

GROWING Hellebores require fertile soil in shade. They prefer not to be moved once planted, so consider their position carefully beforehand. Remove the larger leaves as the buds begin to emerge. Mulch every spring with compost or leafmould.

CUT AND CONDITION Wait until the seedhead has started to form before

cutting hellebores, otherwise the flower will be too immature to stay hydrated. The stem can be quite waxy, so for increased water absorption, score the stem (cutting just 1mm-deep into the outer layer) along the whole length of the stem. If you are cutting when they are a little less mature, the stem ends can be seared in boiling water for 20 seconds.

VASE LIFE Up to two weeks if harvested at the seeded stage.

DRYING No

NOTE The flower heads tend to hang downwards (to protect the nectaries from the winter weather), but some varieties have been bred for upward-facing blooms. Seed-grown hellebores can be very variable so it is advisable to purchase them as pot-grown plants when they are in flower to be assured of the best quality colour and flowers.

Hesperis matronalis / **Sweet rocket** ↑

VARIETIES For white flowers, choose *H. matronalis* var. *albiflora*.

COLOUR Purple and white.

GROWING A biennial that flowers throughout May. Sow seed between May and midsummer; plant out into beds in late summer for flowers the following year. It is tolerant of a range of soils and needs sun or partial shade.

CUT AND CONDITION Stems can be cut just as the first flowers start to open, and flowers will continue to open up the stem once in the vase. Wrap in paper to keep the stems straight.

VASE LIFE 7–10 days

DRYING No

NOTE This is a wonderfully scented bloom and pairs with alliums, cerinthe and lilac for arrangements evocative of springtime cottage gardens. It's an essential choice for filling the May gap.

Leucojum aestivum / Summer snowflake

GROWING This perennial bulb prefers moist, fertile soil in sun for best flower production. Plant bulbs in autumn, or otherwise purchase 'in the green' and plant in the early spring for nodding, white, bell-shaped flowers.

CUT AND CONDITION Harvest as the first buds on the stem open. Pull rather than cut the stems; they exude sap so condition separately as you would for narcissi (see more below and page 131).

VASE LIFE 7–10 days

DRYING No

Malus, *Prunus* and *Pyrus* / Apple, cherry and pear (spring blossom)

CUT AND CONDITION Cut stems when the buds begin to break. Split the stems as for woodies (see page 131) and place into buckets of hot water.

VASE LIFE 5 days

DRYING No

Narcissus / Daffodil →

VARIETIES There are 13 different classes of narcissi, each with their own characteristics, so look into which appeal to you: trumpet, large-cupped, small-cupped, double, triandrus, cyclamineus, jonquilla, tazetta, poeticus, bulbocodium and split corona, plus a further class for those that don't fit into any of the previous categories and another for botanically named species and those found in the wild. There are also hundreds of named varieties to choose from.

COLOUR Mainly yellow, white and cream, with a range of additional cup colours, including peach, pink, red, orange and green.

GROWING Bulbs should be planted into warm soil in the early autumn. They prefer moist but free-draining soil in sun, although they will flower reliably in light shade. Plant a selection of early-, mid- and late-flowering varieties to extend the harvest window from March to May.

CUT AND CONDITION Pull rather than cut the flowering stems to maximise the stem length. All varieties exude a sap that is toxic to other flowers so they must be conditioned separately. Cut the flowers to the required length and then place in a bucket half-filled with water. Change the water a couple of times over the course of a few hours; once the sap has stopped the stems are ready to use. Do not re-cut the stems once conditioned.

VASE LIFE 7 days

DRYING No

NOTE Many varieties are deliciously scented and just a few stems can fill a room with fragrance. The tazetta class have multi-head stems which are highly scented and particularly beautiful, while some of the wild varieties are lovely to use in more naturalistic arrangements.

Opposite *Narcissus* 'Cool Flame' and 'White Lion'

contrast to the other flower shapes usually in bloom at the same time of year. It is the first of the umbellifers to flower, especially if you are able to plant under cover for an April harvest. It is loved by hoverflies and is excellent early fodder for insects.

***Papaver nudicaule* / Icelandic poppy**
GROWING Start the seed in trays in late summer and plant out into beds in autumn. Plants will flower through spring and are an excellent cut-and-come-again crop, providing fruity colours to floral arrangements.
CUT AND CONDITION Cut at the 'cracked bud' stage, just as the casing opens and the petal colour is visible. Sear the stems with a blow torch or in boiling water for a few seconds to extend the vase life.
VASE LIFE 5–7 days
DRYING No

***Orlaya grandiflora* / White laceflower** ↑
COLOUR White
GROWING Orlaya is a hardy annual and late summer-/autumn-sown seeds often provide better quality plants than spring-sown. Sow the seed either directly outside or under cover for flowering the following year. Crops planted in a polytunnel or greenhouse will flower in April, outdoor crops in May. Grow in well-drained soil in sun for the best flowers.
CUT AND CONDITION Cut when the first flower is fully open and the stamens are visible and white – this plant will not hydrate if cut before the stem is fully mature. If the stamens are discoloured the flower will have a shorter vase life. Make sure to cut in cool conditions.
VASE LIFE 7 days
DRYING No
NOTE The lace-like form is a good

***Ranunculus* / Persian buttercup** ↗
VARIETIES Those in the Amandine (pictured), Pauline, Elegance and Cloni series are all bred for cut flowers.
COLOUR Every colour except blue.
GROWING This is a cool-season crop and the corms are usually grown as annuals for the best quality flowers. Start the corms sprouting in autumn; plant them claws down into the soil/compost so the top of the corm is just below the surface. Plant in pots under cover in a polytunnel or greenhouse or in beds outside. Outside plantings may need protection from the worst

winter weather. Consistent watering is required for good flower production.

CUT AND CONDITION Stems should be cut when the bud casing has opened and the head is showing colour. When squeezed, the buds should give like a marshmallow. If they are too hard they won't open fully. Place straight into cool water, but no special conditioning is required.

VASE LIFE 10–14 days

DRYING These are particularly beautiful dried flowers; cut just before they are fully open and dry upside down in the dark to preserve the colour.

NOTE The range of colours and their double, rose-like blooms means these will always be popular. Plant in succession for flowers from March to June: start the first planting in early autumn, the second in early winter and a third in early spring.

**Silene dioica and S. latifolia /
Red campion and white campion** ↑

GROWING This perennial is tolerant of a wide range of soils and growing conditions. Horizontal net support is required as the plant can have a sprawling habit. Cut back after initial flowering to encourage another flush of flowers.

CUT AND CONDITION Allow the first flower on the stem to drop as the first seedhead develops; it will be mature enough to cut as the subsequent flowers begin to open up the stem.

VASE LIFE 7 days

DRYING Seedheads

Syringa vulgaris / **Lilac**

GROWING Lilac requires fertile, well-drained soil in full sun.

CUT AND CONDITION Cut as the first third of the flowers on the panicle are open and remove all of the foliage. Split stems as for woodies (see page 131) and place into buckets of warm water to condition.

VASE LIFE 5–10 days

DRYING No

← *Tulipa* / **Tulip**

VARIETIES There are too many to include here! As with narcissi, there are different classes to explore, including: species, single early/late, lily-flowered, parrot and double early/late.

COLOUR Every colour except true blue.

GROWING Tulips are grown as an annual cut-flower crop. Bulbs should be planted 15cm (6in) deep in free-draining soil after the first frost in late autumn. They can be planted close together but not touching, and you can fit many bulbs into a relatively small space. They grow well in pots, so are suitable for small gardens.

CUT AND CONDITION Singles should be cut when the bud is just showing some colour; they will continue to develop and open in the vase. Parrots and doubles should be almost fully coloured, but not quite open. For all tulips, pull up the whole plant including the bulb. Cut the bulb off and remove all except the top two leaves. Wash the stems, bunch and wrap in paper before placing into a few centimetres of water to condition for a couple of hours before arranging.

VASE LIFE 7–10 days

DRYING No

NOTE Tulips continue to grow in the vase, so cut them a little shorter than usual when arranging as they will grow up through the arrangement. Planting a good selection of early-, mid- and late-season varieties will increase the harvest window, although bear in mind that if there is a hot spell in mid-spring, all of your tulips are likely to come into flower at once.

Viburnum opulus / **Guelder rose**

GROWING These deciduous shrubs are tolerant of a range of conditions but will flower best in full sun, producing gorgeous, white, pompom flower heads. Prune immediately after flowering in order to produce long, straight stems for the following year's flowers.

CUT AND CONDITION Cut the flowers when they are fully open and green, just before they turn white. Split the stem as for woodies (see page 131), place into a bucket of hot water and leave to cool in a dark place.

VASE LIFE 5–10 days

DRYING No

Summer

Summer is sunshine and floral abundance. It's all about the sparkling light, sunflowers stretching towards the sky, soft summer rain and the constant buzz of life in the garden from bees, birds, beetles, busy ants and worms writhing in compost piles. Dancing butterflies and the low drone of dragonflies on the breeze make this one of my favourite times of the year.

ESSENTIAL TASKS

- Sow your biennial varieties so they will be ready to crop next summer. Ideally these should be sown by midsummer to provide a long enough growing period before the winter season sets in.
- Sow the last successions of half-hardy annual varieties for flowering through autumn.
- It's a good time of year to sow perennials so they will be ready for planting out in autumn.
- Keep on top of watering, especially in dry spells of weather. It's particularly important to ensure that new plants and seedlings are well watered while establishing in the garden.
- Feed plants in containers with a high-potash liquid fertiliser throughout summer.
- Ensure that appropriate supports are erected for plants that require them.
- Prune early-summer-flowering woody perennials as soon as they have finished flowering. Check the plant before cutting, but generally these bloom on the previous year's wood, which means that the new growth produced this year will bear flowers next year.
- Start deadheading any varieties that require it: cut-and-come-again plants need to be deadheaded weekly in order to keep up flower production over a long harvest period. Plants such as repeat-flowering roses should be cut back after their first flowering to encourage another flush of blooms.
- Take semi-ripe cuttings of shrubs and woody-stemmed herbs from non-flowering stems. Summer is a great time to increase your stocks of plants like lavender, hydrangea and lavatera using this method of propagation.
- Start to cut stems for drying; any flowers that are not being used fresh for the vase can be cut and bunched to dry for later use (see page 135).

PLANT SUPPORTS

Many plants require some support in the garden and this is especially important if you are growing taller varieties of flowers and you want to ensure the stems remain straight and don't get damaged in windy weather.

If you are growing in a mixed garden border, individual plants can be staked with bamboo canes or heavy-duty wooden stakes. Ornamental metal supports are also useful and decorative in a garden border. If you are growing plants in rows in dedicated cut flower beds then you have a couple of other options open to you.

Above A corral supporting a row of branching sunflowers **Opposite** Netting with a summer crop of ranunculus growing through

Horizontal plant support netting can be erected over plants early in the season – these are held up by wooden posts set at intervals along the length of the bed. The plants will grow up through the netting, which can be moved up the posts as the plants grow, if necessary. Netting is widely available in plastic (which can be reused each year) or in natural materials such as jute. Natural materials do give a little bit and do not remain quite as taut as plastic.

Another method of plant support is corralling. Posts are set around the bed perimeter and rope or baling twine is strung around and across the bed to provide a framework that contains and supports the plants as they grow. It is particularly effective

for larger plants such as branching sunflowers, dahlias and tall perennials like rudbeckia or eupatorium.

All climbing plants require support. Permanent trellis panels can be erected for perennial climbers. Temporary vertical supports made of posts and netting are suitable for annual crops such as sweet peas. Decorative metal supports or wigwams made with lengths of hazel, willow or canes can be used to support climbers in containers or in the ornamental garden.

PINCH PRUNING / CHELSEA CHOP

There are a couple of cultivation techniques that are particularly useful to the cut flower grower. Pinch pruning for annual plants and the Chelsea chop for perennials are two similar processes that produce very effective results.

Both methods have the same aim: to remove the terminal bud of a plant in order to stimulate the lateral buds further down the stem into growth. There are a number of benefits to this process. Instead of one main flowering stem being produced by a plant followed by a later, secondary flush of much lower quality stems, these methods give you a quantity of stems to harvest all at the same flowering stage and of a consistent quality. With many varieties, the primary flowers have very thick stems and huge flower heads which make them unsuitable for cut flower use – pinching or chopping ensures slender stems with smaller blooms that are perfect for arranging. These techniques deliver much better quality plant material that is well suited to the end use.

Pinch prune Annual plants should be pinched when they have formed at least four leaf nodes – this is the point at which lateral buds grow. I usually pinch back my annuals when they reach around 25–30cm (10–12in) in height, well before any flower buds begin to

Pinch pruning the growing tip of an annual, branching helianthus

form and develop. Cut out the leading shoot, and within a few weeks you will see a number of lateral buds growing out from the stem. These laterals will go on to produce lovely, long-stemmed flowers for cutting. It's important to note that pinching will set your harvest window back by two to three weeks, but it's worth the wait for lots more flowers!

PINCH PRUNE ANNUALS

- *Amaranthus* (amaranth)
- *Ammi visnaga* (not *A. majus*, which branches naturally) (toothpick plant)
- *Antirrhinum* (snapdragon)
- *Atriplex* (orache)
- *Bupleurum* (bupleurum)
- *Calendula* (pot marigold)
- *Campanula medium* (Canterbury bells)

Giving perennial rudbeckia 'Henry Eilers' a Chelsea chop to extend the harvest window

Chelsea chop This is used specifically for clump-forming, late-flowering perennial plants. Apical dominance is broken by cutting the developing plant material well before the formation of flower buds. The name is a clue to the best time to carry out this task – at the end of May at the same time that the Chelsea Flower Show is on.

Whatever the height of the perennials you've selected for the chop, take your shears or secateurs and cut the plant material down by half. All of the lateral buds below the cut will be stimulated into growth, producing more stems to harvest with more slender stems and smaller flower heads than plants that have not been cut back. The Chelsea chop will delay flowering for three to four weeks; if you chop some plants and leave others, you can effectively extend your perennial harvest window by a few weeks.

- *Centaurea cyanus* (cornflower)
- *Chrysanthemum* (chrysanthemum)
- *Cosmos* (cosmos)
- *Cynoglossum amabile* (Chinese forget-me-not)
- *Dahlia* (dahlia)
- *Delphinium consolida* (larkspur)
- *Helianthus* (branching) (sunflower)
- *Hesperis* (sweet rocket)
- *Lavatera trimestris* (royal mallow)
- *Malope* (mallow wort)
- *Omphalodes linifolia* (Argentine forget-me-not)
- *Phlox drummondii* (annual phlox)
- *Scabiosa atropurpurea* (sweet scabious)
- *Tanacetum parthenium* (feverfew)
- *Thlaspi* (pennycress)
- *Zinnia* (zinnia)

CHELSEA CHOP PERENNIALS

- *Achillea* (late-flowering) (yarrow)
- *Aster* (including *A.* × *frikartii* and those in the *Symphyotrichum* genus) (Michaelmas daisy)
- *Echinacea* (coneflower)
- *Eryngium* (sea holly)
- *Eupatorium* (Joe-pye weed)
- *Monarda* (bergamot)
- *Penstemon* (penstemon)
- *Phlox* (late-flowering) (phlox)
- *Rudbeckia* (coneflower)
- *Sedum* (stonecrop)
- *Veronicastrum* (culver's root)

Summer flower harvest

Agapanthus / **African lily** →

VARIETIES Lots to choose from: 'Delft Blue' (pictured), 'Midnight Star' and 'Little Dutch White' are all lovely.

COLOUR Mostly blue, with some white and lilac.

GROWING These perennial plants require well-drained soil in full sun. They are excellent plants for container growing. The deciduous varieties tend to be hardier than the evergreen varieties which may need protection through the winter months.

CUT AND CONDITION Cut as the first buds on the head open and place into water.

VASE LIFE 7–10 days

DRYING No

NOTE Some varieties are too large for arranging so check the head size and height before purchasing. There are lots of dwarf varieties that are great for small gardens and their flower heads look lovely tucked into arrangements.

Alchemilla mollis / **Lady's mantle** →

GROWING Grow this perennial in well-drained soil in full sun or part shade.

CUT AND CONDITION Cut when the lime-green flower head is fully open, as it can wilt if it is not mature enough.

VASE LIFE 7–10 days

DRYING The flowers make an interesting dried texture.

Opposite An armful of the beautiful peony 'Catharina Fontijn'

Ammi majus and A. visnaga / False bishop's flower and toothpick plant

VARIETIES *A. majus*: 'Graceland' and 'Queen of Africa'. *A. visnaga*: 'Green Mist' and 'Casablanca'.

COLOUR White

GROWING These hardy annuals can be sown in succession, with one sowing in autumn and subsequent successions starting in spring, giving you flowers right through the summer and autumn. Start in module trays and plant out into beds. *A. visnaga* benefits from pinching to produce straight, slim stems; do not pinch *A. majus* as it branches naturally. Providing support is essential.

CUT AND CONDITION Cut when 75 per cent of the flowers on the head are open but before they start to shed pollen. Place straight into water; *A. majus* requires overnight conditioning before use.

VASE LIFE 5–10 days

DRYING *A. majus* can be air dried.

NOTE This is one of the most popular annual cut flowers and is very easy to grow. Ammi is all romance and light – the quintessential frothy flower that can transform an arrangement.

Antirrhinum / Snapdragon

GROWING These hardy annuals (down to -5°C) can be sown in succession for a harvest in summer and autumn. Sow the tiny seed in trays, prick out into modules and plant out when large enough in well-drained soil in full sun.

CUT AND CONDITION Cut when the first third of the flower head is blooming.

VASE LIFE 7–9 days

DRYING No

Astilbe / Astilbe

GROWING A herbaceous perennial with feather-like plumes of small flowers. Requires fertile soil in partial shade.

CUT AND CONDITION Cut when half of the blooms on the head have opened. Place into buckets of deep, hot water and allow to cool and condition overnight.

VASE LIFE 5–7 days

DRYING Dry flowers or seedheads.

Astrantia / Masterwort ↑

VARIETIES Opt for named varieties rather than species types for more consistent flowering. The Sparkling Stars series, with colours in white, pink and burgundy, are particularly good

with large flowers and plants that produce stems through summer.

COLOUR White, pink and burgundy reds.

GROWING Astrantias are perennial plants that prefer a moisture-retentive soil in partial shade, although they will grow well in sun if they have enough moisture. They are easy to grow and relatively pest and disease free.

CUT AND CONDITION Cut when the uppermost flowers are fully open and the stamens are showing. If cut in bud the stems will wilt.

VASE LIFE 7–10 days

DRYING Hang fully open flowers upside down to air dry.

NOTE These are very popular early summer blooms that grow well in cooler locations where they will continue to produce flowers over a longer period. They provide another interesting texture as a dried stem.

← *Centaurea cyanus* / **Cornflower**

VARIETIES The Classic series provides a good colour range. Also try 'Blue Boy', 'Mauve Ball' (pictured), and 'Black Ball'.

COLOUR Mainly blue, also white through to pink and mauve, and purple-black.

GROWING Sow in autumn for a crop in early summer. Seeds can also be sown through spring for blooms all summer. They need well-drained soil in full sun. Plants require support; they can become tangled and hard to cut if planted too closely together.

CUT AND CONDITION Cut when the flowers are between a quarter and a half open, well before the stamens are exposed. Once the flower is pollinated the vase life will be greatly reduced.

VASE LIFE 5–7 days

DRYING Air dry flowers upside down.

NOTE The traditional blue flowers are the quintessential summer meadow flower and are very popular for wildflower arrangements. The blue can be difficult to pair with other colours, so try growing cornflowers in white, pink or mauve as they are easier to use.

Crocosmia × *crocosmiiflora* / **Montbretia**

GROWING Plant bulbs just a couple of centimetres below the soil surface in spring. Plant a few different varieties to extend the harvest window.

CUT AND CONDITION Cut when the first few fiery flowers on the striking spike swell to coloured buds.

VASE LIFE 7–10 days

DRYING Air dry seedheads.

Daucus carota / **Wild carrot** ↑
VARIETIES 'Dara' (pictured) and
'Purple Kisses'.
COLOUR White through to maroon.
GROWING Similar to ammi, this hardy
annual can be sown in succession for
blooms through summer and autumn.
It branches naturally so there is no
need to pinch prune.
CUT AND CONDITION Cut when the flower
head is almost completely open but
before it begins to shed pollen; place
straight into water. No other special
conditioning required.
VASE LIFE 7 days
DRYING The incurved seedheads make
excellent material for drying.
NOTE Can be susceptible to pests and
diseases that affect the carrot family,
such as carrot root fly and motley virus.
Better plants are produced from direct
sowing as there is less root disturbance.

Delphinium consolida / **Larkspur** →
VARIETIES The QIS and Limelight
series are excellent ('Limelight White'
is pictured). Newer varieties include
'Misty Lavender', 'Smokey Eyes',
'Salmon Beauty' and 'Pink Perfection'.
COLOUR White, pink, mauve, purple
and blue.
GROWING Larkspur can be sown in
succession like other hardy annuals
to extend the harvest period. It can be
sown directly into beds or in modules
to be planted out later. It needs well-
drained soil in sun; make sure that
plants are supported with netting as
they can get blown over in the wind.
CUT AND CONDITION Cut when a third of
the flowers are open on the stem and
place straight into water.
VASE LIFE 7 days
DRYING Cut when most of the flowers
are open on the stem and air dry
upside down.
NOTE Overwintered plants can produce
a rather large initial stem. Pinch this
out when it reaches approximately
30cm (12in); the laterals will grow on to
produce much more usable stems for
floral arranging.

← *Dianthus barbatus* / **Sweet William**

VARIETIES D. barbatus 'Albus' and general mixed varieties are excellent. The Amazon and Hollandia series have both been bred for cut-flower production and can be grown as annuals rather than biennials.

COLOUR White, pink, red, purple, black.

GROWING Sow sweet William seed by midsummer and plant out by early autumn. Plants prefer well-drained soil in sun, and will flower from late May the following year.

CUT AND CONDITION Cut when the first flowers are open on the head and place straight into water; no special conditioning required.

VASE LIFE 10–14 days

DRYING No

NOTE Sweet Williams have a delicious scent and a particularly long vase life. Their stiff stems can be inflexible for arranging and prone to snapping easily, so be gentle with them.

Digitalis / **Foxglove** →

VARIETIES Biennial foxgloves include D. purpurea 'Foxy', 'Snow Thimble', 'Snowy Mountain' and 'Sutton's Apricot'. Perennial foxgloves include those in the Polkadot, Camelot and Dalmatian series, as well as D. × mertonensis and D. obscura 'Sunset'. Those in the Illumination series are not hardy but are stunning.

COLOUR Most colours except true blue and black.

GROWING For biennial foxgloves, seed should be sown by midsummer and planted out by September for flowering the following year. Perennials can be sown in early spring for flowers later in their first year. Foxgloves benefit from afternoon shade; they will tolerate a more sunny aspect as long as they are planted in moisture-retentive soil.

CUT AND CONDITION Cut when a third of the flowers are open on the stem; they will continue to open in the vase. Wrap stems in paper to keep them straight.

VASE LIFE 7–10 days

DRYING The seeded stems after flowering look interesting dried.

NOTE Seed should be sown on the surface of a tray as it requires light to germinate. Seedlings can be pricked out once they are large enough to handle. Search out some of the dwarf varieties with shorter stems as these can be easier to arrange than the very tall varieties.

Place straight into cool water and condition overnight.

VASE LIFE 7 days

DRYING Remove the leaves and petals and dry the central cone of the flower.

NOTE These daisy-like flowers are perfect for wilder arrangements. At the height of summer they are covered with bees, butterflies and hoverflies!

Gillenia / **Bowman's root** →

VARIETIES *G. trifoliata* 'Pink Profusion'.

COLOUR White and pink.

GROWING This herbaceous perennial is best grown in moisture-retentive soil in partial shade, although it will tolerate sun. It is fairly trouble free to grow. It is slow to establish once divided and doesn't like to be moved. Propagate from seed you collect from your plants in autumn – sow the seed in a tray immediately as this species is easier to propagate from fresh seed. Prick out seedlings in spring to grow on.

CUT AND CONDITION Cut as the star-like flowers begin to open; each stem carries an open panicle of many flower buds which will continue to open in the vase.

VASE LIFE 7 days

DRYING The seeded stems dry well.

NOTE Gillenia is not commonly grown but it makes an excellent cut flower and can be used as an alternative to gypsophila. Once the flowers have finished, seeded stems can still be used in arrangements; the red stems and calyces are lovely textural elements In autumn displays as the leaf colour changes.

Echinacea / **Coneflower** ↑

VARIETIES *E. purpurea* 'Magnus' and 'White Swan'. For interesting colours, try 'Green Envy' and those in the Double Scoop series.

COLOUR Mostly pink and white, but there are lots of new varieties being bred in a range of interesting and exciting colours such as coral, orange and green.

GROWING This perennial plant is very easy to grow and tolerant of a range of soil types. It prefers a position in full sun. Sow seed in autumn for planting out the following spring, or divide existing plants in spring. The sturdy stems do not require any further support.

CUT AND CONDITION Cut when the petals are open to a horizontal position and a touch of pollen is showing. If cut too early the flowers will not open fully.

Gladiolus hybrids / **Sword lily**

GROWING Plant bulbs closely in spring and in succession for a long harvest. Prefers well-drained, fertile soil in full sun. Tall varieties need netting support.

CUT AND CONDITION Cut when the first couple of flowers on the spike are open. Keep the stems fully vertical while conditioning or they will bend.

VASE LIFE 7–14 days

DRYING No

← *Helianthus* / **Sunflower**

VARIETIES Single-stemmed varieties include those in the ProCut series and Sunrich series. Branching varieties include 'Valentine', 'Ruby Eclipse' (pictured), 'Soraya' and 'Moulin Rouge'.

COLOUR Yellow, orange, red, maroon.

GROWING Sunflowers are one of the easiest annual plants to grow. Sow the seed in individual cells in a module tray; they will germinate in a few days in ideal conditions and can be planted out into the garden when the risk of frost has passed. Sow sunflowers in succession for a continuous harvest through summer. They need fertile soil with adequate moisture in full sun.

CUT AND CONDITION Cut as soon as the fully coloured petals begin to open and lift off from the centre of the flower bud. You can leave the flower to open fully on the plant, but early cutting reduces the potential for insect damage. Place straight into water.

VASE LIFE 7–10 days

DRYING Dry upside down, with or without petals.

NOTE You can control the head size and the stem thickness of your sunflowers through planting distance: the closer you plant them, the smaller the head. Smaller heads are easier to incorporate into floral designs. Another way to control the head size is through pinching of branching varieties – this also helps to produce a thinner stem which is much easier to arrange with.

Lathyrus odoratus / **Sweet pea**

VARIETIES So many gorgeous varieties: the white 'Jilly', purple 'Nimbus', pale pink 'Mollie Rilstone' and violet 'Noel Sutton' are a few favourites.

COLOUR All colours except bright yellow.

GROWING This climbing annual is perfect for containers in small spaces as well as garden beds. Start the seed in autumn or spring; seed sown in autumn will flower in early summer, or in late spring if planted under cover. Support is essential and plants must be tied in weekly. Deadhead regularly to keep flower production going.

CUT AND CONDITION Cut when the first bloom on the stem has opened and place straight into cool water.

VASE LIFE 3–5 days

DRYING No

NOTE The scent from a handful of sweet peas will fill a room. They can be a labour-intensive crop with continual tying-in, deadheading and feeding required to keep the plants flowering through the summer. Stems will start off long early in the season and gradually shorten as the temperatures rise.

Linaria / **Toadflax** ↑

VARIETIES *L. purpurea* 'Canon Went'
(pictured), 'Peachy' and 'Brown's White
Strain', and *L. maroccana* Licilia series.

COLOUR All colours except true blue.

GROWING Linaria is a short-lived
perennial that is often grown as a hardy
annual. Sow in modules and plant out
in autumn for flowers in early summer.
They are drought-tolerant plants and do
well in free-draining soil in full sun.

CUT AND CONDITION Cut when a third of
the flowers are open on the stem and
place straight into water.

VASE LIFE 7 days

DRYING No

NOTE These dainty, early summer
spikes are perfect for wilder
arrangements and they add a very
garden-like feel to summer florals. The
pink of 'Canon Went' matches that of
the pale pink peony 'Sarah Bernhardt'.

Lysimachia / **Loosestrife** ↑

VARIETIES *L. atropurpurea* 'Beaujolais';
L. clethroides 'Lady Jane' (pictured);
and *L. ephemerum*.

COLOUR Burgundy and white.

GROWING These are vigorous perennials
that can be a bit thuggish in the
garden, so plant with care. They prefer
fertile, moisture-retentive soil in sun
and are fairly trouble free to grow.

CUT AND CONDITION Cut when a third of
the flowers on the head are open and
place straight into water; no special
conditioning required.

VASE LIFE 7–10 days

DRYING No

NOTE The species I've chosen have
an interesting form to add to floral
designs. They flower for 3–4 weeks,
so they are not the longest flowering
perennials, but they are a welcome
addition to the late summer border.

Nigella / Love-in-a-mist ↑

VARIETIES *N. damascena* Miss Jekyll series (pictured) and Persian Jewels Group; *N. papillosa* 'African Bride'; *N. orientalis* 'Transformer' (for seedheads).

COLOUR Blue, white and pink.

GROWING Sow directly in well-drained soil in sun in September. Sow every three weeks through spring for a constant supply of flowers in summer.

CUT AND CONDITION Stems can be cut when the flower bud is fully coloured and just beginning to open. Once the stamens separate away from the centre, vase life will be shorter.

VASE LIFE 5–7 days

DRYING Leave some flowers to develop seedheads for drying. Some varieties are grown specifically for coloured seedheads, such as 'Albion Black Pod'.

NOTE It's easy to sow small patches in between other plants in a border.

Polemonium / Jacob's ladder ↑

VARIETIES *P. caeruleum* f. *album* (pictured), 'Blue Pearl' and 'White Pearl'. Also *P. yezoense* var. *hidakanum* 'Purple Rain' and *P. carneum* 'Apricot Delight'.

COLOUR White, blue, purple, apricot.

GROWING Prefers a semi-shaded spot in moist but well-drained soil. Easy to grow from seed or divide in autumn. Cut back after the first flowers in May/June to encourage another flush.

CUT AND CONDITION Cut as the first flowers on the head open; the remaining buds will continue to open in the vase.

VASE LIFE 7 days

DRYING No

NOTE Polemonium is one of those garden flowers that you won't find commonly as a cut stem, but it lends arrangements a real sense of the garden. The flowers look delicate, but the stems are long and robust.

Rosa / Rose

VARIETIES Too many to mention! Some favourites include 'Lady of Shalott', 'Margaret Merril', 'Queen of Sweden', 'Port Sunlight', 'Chandos Beauty', 'Koko Loco' and 'Blue Moon'.

COLOUR All colours except true blue.

GROWING Roses are woody perennials that require fertile soil in full sun. Buy bare-root or containerised plants from autumn to early spring and plant in a permanent bed. Plants should be pruned to an open goblet shape in winter or early spring. Choose repeat-flowering varieties for flushes of blooms through summer. After the first flush in early summer, cut back to encourage further flowering.

CUT AND CONDITION Cut your roses when they are in bud for the longest vase life – do this when the bud casing has opened and the petals are just beginning to unfurl. Remove any thorns and the lower leaves and split the woody stems (see page 131). Place into a bucket of hot water and leave to condition overnight.

VASE LIFE Variable depending on cutting stage and variety, but generally around 3–6 days.

DRYING Flowers and petals can both be dried.

NOTE It is worth growing a few roses for their scent, despite their relatively short vase life. Save and dry the petals for fragrant bowls of pot pourri. Some varieties have been bred for hip production, and these are useful for autumn/winter arrangements.

← *Scabiosa* / Scabious

VARIETIES *S. atropurpurea* cultivars are grown as annuals or short-lived perennials (such as 'Blue Cockade', pictured); *S. caucasica* is perennial.

COLOUR Every colour from white to black except true blue.

GROWING Both annual and perennial varieties of scabious are easy to grow from seed; sow either in spring or autumn. They require well-drained soil in sun. Deadhead regularly to prevent the plants from going to seed. Support is essential to keep the plants upright and the stems straight.

CUT AND CONDITION Cut as the flowers just begin to unfurl and before the stamens emerge for a longer vase life.

VASE LIFE 6–8 days

DRYING Air dry seedheads.

NOTE These make excellent filler flowers, and their wide colour range means that they are particularly useful for floral arranging. They add a lovely textural element with small heads on long, fine stems. Scabious is very versatile and equally at home in wildflower displays and more formal arrangements.

Herbs

I love using herbs to arrange with. From the fresh green leaves of apple mint to the tiny flowers of oregano, they bring the element of scent to floral work. Some herbs such as lavender and rosemary are already widely used in floristry, but there are some that are more unusual and easy to grow in our gardens.

Most herbs are ready to cut through the summer months, but many can also be dried for use in winter. They comprise all of the plant types – annuals, perennials and woody-stemmed – and they make for great foliage and filler material.

ANNUALS
- *Anethum graveolens* (dill)
- *Basilicum* (basil)
- *Tanacetum parthenium* (feverfew)

PERENNIALS
- *Allium schoenoprasum* (chive)
- *Aloysia citrodora* (lemon verbena)
- *Foeniculum* (fennel)
- *Mentha* (mint)
- *Monarda* (bergamot)
- *Origanum* (oregano)
- *Pelargonium* (scented-leaf) (pelargonium)

WOODY-STEMMED
- *Laurus nobilis* (bay)
- *Lavandula* (lavender)
- *Salvia* (sage)
- *Salvia rosmarinus* (rosemary)

Top A handful of lavender **Bottom** A vase of flowering oregano

Lavandula / Lavender

VARIETIES Look for long-stemmed varieties for arranging, such as *L. × intermedia* 'Grosso', 'Vera' or 'Lullingstone Castle', as well as *L. angustifolia* 'Hidcote'.

COLOUR Mostly mauve and purple, plus some white and pink.

GROWING All lavenders require full sun and well-drained soil. They perform poorly and are short-lived on heavy soils. Trim back all growth in early spring but take care not to cut back into the old wood. If plants are trimmed back after the first flowering, a second flush may occur in September.

CUT AND CONDITION Cut as the first blooms on the head begin to open. Cutting for drying must be done at the early stage as mature heads will shed.

VASE LIFE 5–7 days

DRYING Hang in bunches upside down.

NOTE Lavender is a great fragrant cut, and is an excellent dried flower for use in the winter with a scent redolent of hot summer days. It is particularly good worked into dried wreaths, either with other plants or on its own.

Mentha / Mint ↗

VARIETIES Look for varieties with an upright growth habit and long stem length. *M. suaveolens* (apple mint) is invaluable, as is *M. × piperita* f. *citrata* 'Chocolate' (chocolate peppermint). Also *M. longifolia* Buddleia Mint Group and *M. suaveolens* 'Variegata' (pineapple mint), which has white variegation on the leaves.

Top and bottom Grow different varieties of mint for a range of scents and flower colours

COLOUR Green foliage; at flowering time mint flowers display a range of whites, pale pinks and mauves.

GROWING Contrary to common advice on growing herbs in impoverished ground (for better flavour), herbs grown for cut flowers need fertile soil. Mint in particular responds well to soil with high fertility that has been conditioned with a deep mulch of compost. Regular watering is essential for leaf crops. Mint also needs support (apple mint can grow to over 1.5m/5ft high!), so install a layer of netting for best results. Mint has running roots and can spread, so grow in containers or be prepared to cut back the runners each year. A little afternoon shade can be helpful in preserving the quality of the stems.

CUT AND CONDITION Foliage can be cut as soon as it is mature enough to stay hydrated. You will notice a hardening of the stem as it matures and this will be at slightly different times in the season for each variety (apple mint can be cut from May, peppermint from late June). At the foliage stage, stems need to be wrapped and placed in deep water overnight to fully condition. Once in flower the stems are fully mature and require very little conditioning.

VASE LIFE 7–10 days

DRYING Flower heads can be dried.

NOTE Mint is the workhorse of the cutting garden, producing stems right through the growing season and adding another green texture for use in arranging. It's one of my favourite plants to grow.

Origanum / **Oregano** ↓

VARIETIES 'Kent Beauty', 'Aureum' and *O. laevigatum* 'Hopleys' .

COLOUR White, pale pink and mauve.

GROWING Requires well-drained soil in full sun, with plenty of organic matter in the soil. It's easy to grow and doesn't require any support.

CUT AND CONDITION Cut as the first blooms open on the flower head and place straight into water. No special conditioning required.

VASE LIFE 7 days

DRYING Dry the heads once the flowers have finished for an interesting texture.

NOTE Most varieties have an upright habit, producing long, straight stems. 'Kent Beauty' is very different: it is a dwarf variety that has soft pink, hop-like flowers that are wonderful for small summer arrangements.

Autumn

Autumn is rich with colour and texture: grasses shimmering in the low evening light, the soft rays of the golden hour on jewel-toned dahlias, and dewdrops on spider webs spun between stems. This is the season of warm days, cool nights, flocks of chattering finches and the hope that autumn's first frost doesn't come too soon. It's the time to gather and store seed for next year's flowers, to plant bulbs deep in the earth for blooms the following spring, and to plan ahead while savouring the last garden flowers of the year.

ESSENTIAL TASKS

- In early autumn, plant out biennials and hardy annuals sown in late summer for an early crop of flowers next year. They need plenty of time to establish a good root system before the winter weather sets in.
- Plant bulbs of spring-flowering varieties. Narcissi, fritillaries, anemones and ranunculus should be planted in September and October; leave the tulips to be planted in late November after the first frost has cooled the soil to help prevent disease such as tulip fire.
- Plant bulbs in layers in pots for a continual spring harvest.
- Start to plant prepared bulbs (those that have been through a cold treatment to trigger growth) in pots in succession for forcing into flower

through the winter months for indoor displays. Suitable bulbs include narcissus, hyacinth and amaryllis.
- Lift any tender plants, including dahlias, if you are on heavy soil. Do this well before any anticipated cold weather. Store the tender plants or tubers somewhere dry and frost free.
- Take cuttings from tender plants such as salvias and pelargoniums to propagate them. They can overwinter in a frost-free place.
- Take hardwood cuttings from trees and shrubs to increase your stocks of woody foliage material.
- Save seed from your favourite flowers. Certain plants — orlaya for instance — germinate readily from freshly saved seed, while germination of older seed can be erratic as it may have gone into dormancy. Some varieties are promiscuous and the colour range from a batch of saved seed may not be true to type, but you may discover a whole new colour!
- Lift and divide early-flowering perennial plants so they have time to establish their roots before winter.
- Remove the mature leaves of hellebores as the flowering stems begin to emerge.
- Ensure that your dried flowers are kept in a place that is free from damp air; you need to prevent the dried stems from absorbing any moisture as it will cause the stems to rot.

Autumn flower harvest

Anemone × hybrida / **Japanese anemone** →

VARIETIES 'Honorine Jobert', 'Robustissima', 'Queen Charlotte' and 'Serenade' (pictured), as well as *A. hupehensis* 'Pocahontas'.

COLOUR White and pink.

GROWING Japanese anemones are spreading herbaceous perennials that require shade and a fertile, well-drained soil. They are woodland plants so are tolerant of dry soils. They dislike being moved, but can be propagated easily by root cuttings.

CUT AND CONDITION Cut as the petals separate and the flower begins to open. Once the stamens are flat and dull against the petals, the flower is too mature to cut. Only cut in cool conditions and place immediately into deep, cool water to condition overnight.

VASE LIFE 4–5 days

DRYING Air dry seedheads.

NOTE Japanese anemones add a sense of movement to autumn displays. Their short vase life means they are only really suitable for event arrangements as they won't last the week.

← *Cosmos bipinnatus* / **Cosmea**

VARIETIES 'Purity', 'Sea Shells', 'Xanthos' and 'Cupcakes'. Also those in the Double Click series (pictured), as well as *C. sulphureus* 'Diablo'.

COLOUR White, pink, burgundy, yellow and orange.

GROWING Sow a succession of this half-hardy annual in spring for a continuous supply of flowers through summer and autumn. They require fertile soil in full sun and support such as netting. Pinch plants when they reach 25–30cm (10–12in) tall. They will continue to produce flowers until the first frost if they are deadheaded regularly.

CUT AND CONDITION Cut just as the coloured bud begins to open for the longest vase life and place straight into cool water to condition overnight.

VASE LIFE 5–7 days

DRYING No

NOTE The double varieties (try the Double Click series) have a longer vase life than the singles. Grow a selection for a range of different flower shapes.

Eupatorium maculatum /
Joe-pye weed →

VARIETIES *E. dubium* 'Little Joe' has a
more compact form.

COLOUR Dusky pink

GROWING A herbaceous perennial that
requires moisture-retentive soil in sun.
It is easy to grow and does not require
additional support. Use the Chelsea
chop technique (see page 83) to
extend the harvest season.

CUT AND CONDITION Cut as the central
buds on the head swell, but just before
the flowers fully open. Place straight
into cool water.

VASE LIFE 7 days

DRYING No

NOTE The colour blends beautifully
with dahlias and cosmos, adding
another textural bloom to the autumn
palette. This plant is an insect magnet.
Dwarf varieties such as 'Little Joe' or
'Baby Joe' are good for small gardens;
note that *E. maculatum* can reach over
1.8m (6ft) tall!

← *Gladiolus murielae* /
Abyssinian gladiolus

COLOUR White with a burgundy blotch.

GROWING This bulb is not reliably
perennial and is best treated as an
annual. The bulbs should be planted
into warm soil, so wait until late spring
and then plant 10–15cm (4–6in) deep.
They need to be planted in full sun.
Plants may be slow to start, but the
sword-like foliage will grow quickly
once it emerges. Flowering stems
will be ready to harvest in autumn.

CUT AND CONDITION Cut as the first
flower in the spike begins to open;
no special conditioning required.
Subsequent buds will open in the vase.

VASE LIFE 7–10 days

DRYING No

NOTE These lovely autumn flowers are
a complete contrast to the colourful,
stiff stems of dahlias and rudbeckias.
Their graceful movement adds
interest and lightness to autumnal
arrangements, while their scent offers
yet another dimension.

Hesperantha coccinea / Crimson flag lily

VARIETIES *H. coccinea* f. *alba* has a white flower head, 'Major' is pinky-red, 'Jennifer' is pale pink and 'Fenland Daybreak' a vivid salmon shade.

COLOUR Coral red, pink and white.

GROWING A perennial plant that produces striking spikes of star-shaped flowers. It is easy to grow in fertile, moist soil in sun. Grow from seed sown in spring, or buy as young plants and plant in spring. Plants can be divided to increase your stocks in spring as the soil starts to warm up.

CUT AND CONDITION Cut as soon as the first buds on the stem open; the remaining buds will continue to open in the vase. Place into water; no special conditioning required.

VASE LIFE 7 days

DRYING No

NOTE Hesperantha will flower quite late into the autumn in a palette of colours that pair well with the dahlias. Their lovely linear form and star-shaped blooms provide a good textural contrast to the rounded shapes of the dahlias.

Nerine bowdenii / Bowden lily ↗

VARIETIES 'Alba', 'Patricia' and 'Zeal Giant'.

COLOUR Pink and white.

GROWING Plant these perennial bulbs in spring or autumn in well-drained soil in sun, with the tips of the bulbs showing just above the surface of the soil. They also grow well in containers.

They take a couple of seasons to settle in, but once they clump up they should flower reliably in sunny spots.

CUT AND CONDITION Cut stems just as the buds begin to open; no special conditioning required.

VASE LIFE 7–10 days

DRYING No

NOTE These autumn-flowering bulbs provide a hit of colour late in the season. Their blooms look delicate but they are remarkably robust. There are a number of tender varieties which can be grown under cover in a greenhouse or polytunnel, but *N. bowdenii* includes the only reliably hardy varieties.

Nicotiana / Tobacco plant

VARIETIES Lots to choose from including *N. langsdorffii* cultivars, *N. × hybrida* 'Whisper Mixed' and 'Tinkerbell', *N. alata* cultivars and *N. mutabilis.*

COLOUR All colours except true blue.

GROWING Nicotiana is actually a short-lived perennial, but is best treated as a half-hardy annual. The seeds are tiny and should be sown thinly on the surface of the soil from mid-April. Prick out seedlings into individual cells in a module tray and grow on. Harden off and plant out in the garden once the risk of frost has passed. Prefers a position in moisture-retentive soil in full sun and will flower from late summer until the first frosts of autumn.

CUT AND CONDITION Cut as the first flowers on the stem begin to open and place straight into water. No special conditioning required.

VASE LIFE 7 days

DRYING No

NOTE Nicotiana is a cut-and-come-again plant, and it will keep producing flowering stems as long as you keep cutting. It does well in pots so is a great choice for small spaces. The lovely evening scent and delicate form of the flowers make it an excellent late-season cutting plant.

Rudbeckia / Coneflower ↑

VARIETIES My favourite perennial is *R. subtomentosa* 'Henry Eilers' (pictured). Other good perennials include *R. fulgida* var. *sullivantii* 'Goldsturm' and *R. laciniata* 'Herbstsonne'. Annuals include *R. hirta* 'Sahara', 'Cherry Brandy', 'Cherokee Sunset' and 'Prairie Sun'.

COLOUR Yellow, orange, russet and red.

GROWING All types prefer moisture-retentive soil in sun. If dividing perennials, do so in spring. Sow half-hardy annuals in mid- to late-spring and plant out after the risk of frost.

CUT AND CONDITION Cut all varieties when the flowers are fully open but before they are fully pollinated.

VASE LIFE Perennials 7–10 days; annuals: 5–7 days

DRYING No

NOTE The sunset tones of 'Sahara' make

it an almost perfect autumnal bloom
– it can be a little temperamental and
difficult to hydrate though. Searing the
stem ends in boiling water for a few
seconds can help, but make sure the
flower heads are mature enough before
cutting. The perennials are easy and
trouble free to grow and cut.

Symphyotrichum /
Michaelmas daisy →

VARIETIES Familiar to many as
asters, the daisy-like flowers in the
Symphyotrichum genus include the
classic pale purple 'Little Carlow',
and the cerise 'Rose Queen', plus *S.
ericoides* 'Pink Cloud' (pictured) and
S. novi-belgii 'White Ladies', though
there are many more to choose from.
COLOUR White, pink, mauve and purple.
GROWING Autumn-flowering
Michaelmas daisies are herbaceous
perennials that do best in well-drained
soil in part shade. They require more
moisture if grown in full sun. Divide
plants in spring if required. This crop
benefits from the Chelsea chop (see
page 83) and some support.
CUT AND CONDITION Cut as the first
few blooms open on the flower head
and place into water. No special
conditioning required.
VASE LIFE 7–10 days
DRYING No
NOTE Select a few different varieties
to spread the harvest period through
September and October. They provide
a delightful textural contrast to large-
flowered dahlias.

Xerochrysum bracteatum / **Strawflower** ↙

VARIETIES 'Apricot Peach Mix', 'Pomegranate', 'Silvery Rose', 'Dragon Fire', plus various mixed choices.

COLOUR All colours except true blue.

GROWING Sow annual seed in autumn or spring; plant out in well-drained soil in full sun. Plants require support.

CUT AND CONDITION Cut just as the blooms start to unfurl and before they are fully open. Place straight into water to condition.

VASE LIFE 7–10 days

DRYING Dry upside down in bunches, or wire the individual flower heads.

NOTE This is the quintessential dried flower, also known by its previous name, helichrysum, as well as the common name everlasting. The papery texture when fresh gives a hint to its potential longevity. The colour range blends beautifully with the jewel tones of autumn dahlias.

Zinnia elegans / **Zinnia**

VARIETIES Opt for those in the Benary's Giant, Queen, Lilliput and Zinderella series.

COLOUR All colours except black and true blue.

GROWING Zinnias prefer well-drained soil and full sun; they do not perform well in cool, damp conditions. They are half-hardy annuals, so sow seed under cover in late spring and do not plant out until all risk of frost has passed. The plants should be pinched when they reach around 30cm (12in) – this will encourage the production of lots of flowering stems. They will flower from late summer until the first frosts in autumn.

CUT AND CONDITION Cut when the flower is fully open. Give the stem a wiggle and if it stays firm and straight it is ready to cut, but if the stem is floppy it is not yet mature enough to stay hydrated. Place straight into water.

VASE LIFE 7 days

DRYING No

NOTE Zinnias, like dahlias, just get better the more you cut them. Go for a variety of large and small flower sizes to add layers of depth and interest to your autumn floral arrangements.

Dahlia / Dahlia

VARIETIES Dahlias are classified into 14 different groups, all of which have different qualities for the vase, so it's worth researching the ones that appeal to you. They are grouped as follows: single-flowered, anemone-flowered, collerette, waterlily, formal decorative, ball, pompon, cactus, semi-cactus, miscellaneous, fimbriated, star, double orchid and peony.

COLOUR Dahlias come in every colour (except true blue) and a wide range of shapes and forms, which makes them exceptional for floral arranging.

GROWING Dahlias are the stars of the autumn cutting garden. They start to flower in late summer and will continue to bloom until the first frosts bring the season to a close. They are relatively easy to grow. Depending on your location they may not be completely hardy and plants will need to be started from tubers or cuttings each spring. If you have a greenhouse (or somewhere to grow them where they can be protected from frost) you can start growing tubers in early spring, otherwise wait until after the last spring frost to plant tubers straight into the garden – this is usually in May.

Tubers have multiple growing points around the collar called 'eyes' and flowering stems are produced from these growing points. If your tuber

Top *Dahlia* 'Preference'
Bottom *Dahlia* 'Karma Prospero'
Opposite Ball dahlias such as 'Cornel Brons' have the longest vase life

115

does not have an eye it will not sprout and produce a viable plant. Eyes can be difficult to see clearly in autumn/winter, but can be identified as small bumps around the collar of the tuber. As temperatures rise through spring, it becomes easier to spot viable eyes beginning to sprout as they swell on the collar. These sprouts will be either green or red-purple in colour depending on the leaf colour of the variety.

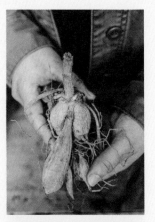

Tubers can be potted up using multi-purpose compost; place the tuber so it sits just below the soil surface. Water well once the tuber has been initially potted, but don't water again until you see the shoots emerging (too much water at this stage can cause the tubers to rot). Grow in a frost-free place, then harden the plants off a couple of weeks before you are ready to plant them out once all risk of frost has passed. Plants will start to flower in late summer.

Dahlias prefer to grow in fertile soil in full sun with a little shelter from the wind. They are heavy-feeding plants, and may benefit from an additional application of fertiliser at planting time. I plant my dahlias 50cm (20in) apart in cutting beds. Once planted, water frequently until the plants are established, especially in periods of dry weather. Plants should receive consistent watering – it's better to give them a deep watering once a week rather than little and often.

Pinch out the growing tip to produce a sturdy, bushy and more floriferous plant

Earwigs, slugs and snails, aphids and thrips are all elements of the garden ecosystem that can cause problems with dahlias, so vigilance and some protection will be required for blemish-free blooms.

Dahlias will keep producing blooms until the end of the season, so deadhead any flowers that you have not cut for the vase on a weekly basis.

OVERWINTER Dahlias should be lifted and stored over winter if your soil is heavy; on lighter sandy soils it is possible to leave them in the ground over the winter months. They can tolerate freezing temperatures, but excessive winter wet will cause the tubers to rot. If tubers are to be left in the ground in winter, a deep mulch of straw or compost can help to insulate them against low temperatures.

Once the plants are growing well and the shoots reach 25–30cm (10–12in), pinch out the growing tip to encourage them to bush out and produce further flowering stems. The larger growing varieties require some support: individual plants in borders can be supported with canes or wooden stakes; and rows of plants in cutting beds can be supported with horizontal netting or be corralled using posts and rope.

Dahlias make excellent container plants, but make sure they are planted into a rich growing medium that will support their growth through the season. Plants in pots may require additional liquid feed later in the summer and autumn. A cane inserted into each pot can support the plant as it grows.

If you are lifting tubers, wait until after they have been frosted and the foliage turns black as this cures and hardens them in preparation for storage. Cut the stems down to about 10cm (4in) from the ground, then dig the tuber out. Brush off the excess soil and place the tubers upside down indoors to dry out for a couple of weeks. Once dry, the tubers should be stored in crates or boxes and packed into a medium such as dry compost. Place somewhere frost-free for the winter. Make sure to check the tubers while in storage and dispose of any tubers that begin to rot.

Unusual forms such as 'Honka Fraqile' have a short vase life but are loved by pollinators

Dahlias in a vase: 'Burlesca' (bottom left), 'Jowey Winnie' (centre) and 'Preference' (top right)

Unpack carefully in spring when it's time to start growing again. Dahlias can be divided when they come out of storage to increase your stocks; make sure that each division has at least one eye visible to ensure it will make a viable plant.

CUT AND CONDITION Dahlias shouldn't be cut in bud as they will not open in the vase like some other flowers. The optimum cutting stage for a dahlia is when the flower is 75 per cent open, before it is fully reflexed and the outer petals begin to droop. Stems should be cut in the cool of the morning and placed straight into water; some people swear by searing their dahlias in hot water, but I never do. They always hydrate well for me when conditioned simply in buckets of deep, cool water.

VASE LIFE Dahlias generally have a shorter vase life than many other flowers; ball and pompon types have the longest life at around 5–6 days, with the singles at around 3 days. They also have 'dirty stems' which means that they sour the water quickly, so care must be taken to change the water frequently (see page 133). Despite all this, they make excellent specimens and are an essential component of autumn arrangements.

DRYING It's worth trying to dry dahlia stems by hanging them upside down – they make amazing dried stems, but they do take a long time to fully dry.

119

Grasses and seedheads

Autumn is the season when all of the textural elements of the garden come into play. Grasses, seedheads and grains such as atriplex bring a sense of the seasonal harvest to arrangements. From the bottlebrush-like heads of pennisetum to the airy panicles of panicum, there is a range of plant shapes, sizes and textures to add layers of interest to autumn displays.

There is a variety of both annual and perennial grasses to choose from for the cutting garden. Large, upright plants like calamagrostis provide long stems for statement pieces, and their flower heads can also be dried for amazing specimens to use through the winter months. *Chasmanthium latifolium* (northern sea oats) is a florists' favourite, with thin, gracefully arching stems and flattened heads that bring light and movement.

Most annual and perennial grasses prefer growing in well-drained soil in full sun. They will supply a huge number of stems per plant and many are excellent for growing in containers in small spaces. Most perennial grasses can be divided to increase your stocks in late spring or early summer. This must be done while the soil is warm and not in autumn/winter. Leave stems to provide interest in winter, and cut back foliage in late winter or early spring before the new season's growth emerges.

ANNUALS (OR TREAT AS ANNUALS)

- *Amaranthus caudatus* (love-lies-bleeding)
- *A. cruentus* (prince's feather)
- *Atriplex hortensis* (garden orache)
- *Avena sativa* (oat)
- *Briza maxima* (greater quaking grass)
- *Hordeum jubatum* (foxtail barley)
- *Lagurus ovatus* (hare's tail grass)
- *Lepidium sativum* (garden cress)
- *Linum usitatissimum* (common flax)
- *Panicum elegans* (switch grass)
- *Papaver* sp. (poppy)
- *Pennisetum glaucum* (African millet)
- *P. orientale* (oriental fountain grass)
- *P. setaceum* (fountain grass)
- *Phalaris canariensis* (canary grass)
- *Setaria italica* (foxtail millet)
- *Sorghum bicolor* (common sorghum)
- *Thlaspi arvense* (field pennycress)
- *Triticum aestivum* (bread wheat)

PERENNIALS

- *Briza media* (common quaking grass)
- *Calamagrostis brachytricha* (Korean feather reed grass)
- *Chasmanthium latifolium* (northern sea oats)
- *Cortaderia selloana* (pampas grass)
- *Miscanthus* sp. (silver grass)
- *Panicum virgatum* (switch grass)
- *Pennisetum alopecuroides* (Chinese fountain grass)
- *P. villosum* (feathertop)
- *Stipa gigantea* (golden oats)

Chasmanthium latifolium / Northern sea oats

VARIETIES 'River Mist' is a white-variegated variety.

COLOUR Green, with flower heads turning bronze.

GROWING This spreading perennial grass prefers a slightly moist soil in either sun or partial shade. Sow seed in spring, otherwise plants can be purchased and planted through the year. Divide plants in late spring/early summer.

CUT AND CONDITION Cut when the flowers are fully formed. Place straight into water or bunch and hang to dry.

VASE LIFE 10 days

NOTE This has long been used by florists and adds a wonderful sense of movement and light to arrangements. It has unusual flattened panicles of flowers which turn from fresh green to bronze as autumn temperatures drop.

Miscanthus sinensis / Chinese silver grass ↗

VARIETIES Dwarf varieties include 'Yakushima Dwarf', 'Starlight' and 'Little Kitten'. Larger varieties include 'Ferner Osten' and 'Dronning Ingrid'. *M. nepalensis* has gracefully drooping heads.

COLOUR Silver, gold, pink and burgundy.

GROWING Miscanthus prefers a well-drained soil in full sun for the best flowers and is very easy to grow. Sow seeds or divide plants in spring. Dwarf

varieties grow well in pots, but most miscanthus grow into large specimens so give them plenty of space.

CUT AND CONDITION Cut when the flower heads are fully open and place straight into water. Bunch and hang if drying.

VASE LIFE 10 days

NOTE I prefer to use as a dried stem rather than fresh; the texture of the head develops as it dries, leaving a light, fluffy head that holds its form and does not shed like pampas grass. It makes a statement on its own in a vase as well as providing an interesting texture in mixed dried arrangements.

Pennisetum / **Fountain grass** ↑

VARIETIES Annuals include *P. advena* 'Rubrum' and *P. setaceum* 'Fireworks'. Perennials include *P. alopecuroides* 'Hameln' and 'Dark Desire' (pictured), *P. thunbergii* 'Red Buttons' and *P. villosum*.

COLOUR Green, gold, pink and bronze.

GROWING Whether annual or perennial, all fountain grasses prefer a well-drained but fertile soil in sun. Sow seed or divide plants in spring.

CUT AND CONDITION Cut when the flower head is fully formed. Place straight into water or bunch and hang for drying.

VASE LIFE 7–10 days

NOTE Pennisetum produces flowers in many sizes and forms, from the stiff spikes of 'Dark Desire' to the gracefully arching 'Rubrum'. The colour range makes it very versatile, and the flower heads fade to a lovely buff shade when dry.

Setaria italica / **Foxtail millet** ↑

VARIETIES 'Hylander', 'Red Jewel' and *S. viridis* 'Caramel' (pictured).

COLOUR Green, red and bronze.

GROWING Setaria is very easy to grow. Sow annual seed in succession for a harvest in summer and autumn. Sow a pinch of seeds in each cell of a module tray and cover lightly with vermiculite. Harden off and plant out once risk of frost has passed. Plant out at 15cm (6in) spacing in well-drained soil in sun.

CUT AND CONDITION Cut once the seedheads are fully formed and extend from the leaf shaft; either place straight into water or bundle to air dry.

VASE LIFE 7–10 days

NOTE 'Caramel' is a fine variety with small heads; 'Hylander' is a useful vertical element for autumn displays. All provide plenty of seed which birds love, so leave a few stems through winter.

Winter

As the seasons take the final turn of the year, the garden settles down to the quiet dormancy of winter. The bones of the garden are exposed, new plans are made, seed catalogues perused. It's time to cut back the plants and clear the beds; bright, cold days spent working in the garden are followed by evenings arranging the abundance of dried flowers that were picked fresh in summer. The golden tones of dried grasses and seedheads remind us of summer's warmth and winter gives us time to sit back and revel in the intricacies and textures of our dried floral material before spring returns with the promise of another year of flowers.

ESSENTIAL TASKS

- Clear annual beds of any spent plant material and prepare no-dig beds for the coming season by adding a layer of compost or other organic matter (see page 62).
- Protect any plants that are not fully hardy with a deep mulch of straw, compost or bark to provide an extra layer of insulation from the winter weather.
- Cut down the foliage of herbaceous perennials to ground level and compost the material. Leave grasses to be cut back in spring.
- Roses should be pruned back to a framework in winter. Use the 'three Ds' method as a guide: cut back any dead, dying or diseased stems first. Then remove any crossing stems and prune to develop an open goblet shape which will improve airflow and reduce the risk of disease. This regime should help to produce long, straight stems which are suitable for floristry use, without thicket-like, twiggy growth.
- Plant bare-root roses and shrubs through the dormant season.
- Take root cuttings of varieties such as *Anemone × hybrida* (Japanese anemones), eryngiums and phlox for propagating.
- Keep a check on your overwintering hardy annuals; cover with netting or fleece to protect them from potential pests or to give a little protection from winter winds.
- During a dry spell plants such as biennials and hardy annuals may need to be watered, so check on them in dry weather and water accordingly; do not water if very low temperatures are forecast.
- Check on stored bulbs and tubers for signs of rot.

04

Care

Learn to condition and arrange your flowers

Cutting and conditioning flowers

Going out to the garden to cut flowers that I have grown is always an exciting prospect. I want my flowers to give me their absolute best in the vase, which means they need to be cut and then conditioned carefully to ensure the longest vase life possible.

CUTTING STAGE

As soon as a stem is cut it begins to senesce – this is the biochemical process by which the flower matures and deteriorates with age. We try to prolong the life of a cut flower by placing it straight into water to keep it hydrated until it eventually dies.

Every variety or species has its own specific cutting stage – this is the optimum moment for cutting that will give you the longest possible vase life. There are a few rules and tips to bear in mind but, overall, knowing the cutting stage is just a matter of learning what works best for each type of flower you grow.

- For a vast number of flowers, the optimum cutting stage is when the bud is just beginning to show colour, but care must be taken not to cut too early as the bud may be too immature to continue to develop in the vase.

- Flowers such as peonies and ranunculus, for example, should be cut at what is called the 'marshmallow stage' – that is, when the bud is showing colour, but is squishy like a marshmallow when squeezed. They won't open properly in the vase if cut when the buds are hard to the touch.

- For plants that flower in spikes, such as delphiniums and foxgloves, cut when the bottom third of flowers on the spike are open.

- For flowers that form umbels, cut when approximately half the flowers on the head are open.

- If a flower is over-mature and in full bloom, it will likely go over in the vase very quickly as it has passed the optimum point for cutting. However, certain varieties must be cut when they are fully open as they will not continue to open in the vase – bupleurum, dahlias and celosia are key examples.

- The maturity of the flower head is not the only consideration; it is also important that the stem has the ability to take up water once cut and remain well hydrated. Immature stems will begin to wilt because they are not able to take up water in the same way as a mature stem.

CUTTING

There are a few things to be aware of before you go out into the garden and start cutting the flowers you've worked so hard to grow.

- Prepare a clean bucket and fill with a few centimetres of water – and when I say clean, I mean clean enough to drink out of! The bucket should be carried out with you into the garden before you start cutting.
- Ensure that you use a clean, sharp pair of floristry scissors or secateurs. Needlenose-type pruners or secateurs are much more useful for cutting than traditional secateurs as their pointed blades are more suited to fine work; heavier secateurs can be used for cutting dense, woody stems. Choose a cutting tool that is light and fits your hand comfortably.
- It's best to cut your flowers during the coolest time of the day – either in the early morning or in the evening – particularly at the height of summer. If cut in the heat of the day some varieties will be extremely difficult to hydrate and heat stress can adversely affect vase life. Grasses and seedheads are more tolerant of higher temperatures.
- Stems should be cut at a 45-degree angle to allow for maximum surface area exposure for the take up of water (pictured, top). Take care to cut in a way that does not cause damage to the plant. Cut above a bud on cut-and-come-again plants and woody

plants to encourage them to continue to be productive and produce further stems for cutting.
- Stems should immediately be placed into your clean bucket of water.

CONDITIONING

Conditioning is the process of preparing the stems and allowing them to rest and rehydrate in water once they have been cut. It's very simple but essential, and ensures that your harvest of flowers performs at its best in the vase. Many people don't realise just how important and effective conditioning can be in prolonging vase life: flowers cut at midday and plonked into a vase on a table in a warm kitchen probably won't last a day – they will start to wilt or twist as they try to rehydrate under stress. Take care to condition your stems and you will increase vase life and your enjoyment of the flowers.

- Once you have cut your stems at the coolest time of day put them straight into a bucket of water.
- Strip the stems of any foliage that will sit below the water line, and if necessary re-cut them under water before placing them into another clean bucket – this time filled high with water – to fully rehydrate.
- Place your bucket somewhere cool and dark to reduce transpiration for at least a few hours, after which your stems will be well conditioned and ready to use. If you are able to leave them overnight and arrange your stems the next day, so much the better.

SPECIAL CONDITIONING

Some varieties and stem types require some special conditioning tricks to maintain quality and extend their vase life.

Wrapping Some varieties can bend and twist as they hydrate, leaving stems difficult to arrange. Once you have stripped away any leaves, secure a number of stems together with a band or tie, then wrap in paper to ensure the stems stay straight while conditioning. Tulips, snapdragons and mint are flowers that benefit from wrapping to maintain straight stems.

Searing Poppies, hellebores and cerinthe, among others, are plants that can be hard to hydrate and benefit from searing when cut in order to prepare the stems for the vase. Searing can either be done by burning the cut stem ends with a flame burner or by dipping them into a cup of boiling water for a few seconds. The stems should then be placed straight into a bucket of cool water to condition as normal – you'll be amazed at how they perk up once they've had this treatment. This technique should only be used for solid-stemmed varieties.

Splitting woody stems Woody stems need to have the surface area of the stem increased for maximum take-up of water. Once the stem has been cut at a 45-degree angle, make a second perpendicular cut approximately 2.5cm (1in) up the stem effectively creating a split which increases the surface area (pictured on page 129). Never hammer woody stems – this traditional practice damages the ends of the xylem vessels, impeding the uptake of water and increasing the potential for bacterial growth.

Hot water treatment Lots of flowering woody stems can be temperamental and difficult to hydrate. Hydrangea, philadelphus and lilac are some of the woody plants that hydrate better if the stems are placed into buckets filled high with hot water, and then left to cool to room temperature. The hot water pushes any air bubbles out of the denser stems which allows unimpeded movement of water up the stem.

Toxic stem sap Euphorbia releases a sap when cut that can be an irritant, so care must be taken to protect your skin from the latex. The stems of varieties that exude sap should be cut to size and then seared before arranging – do not re-cut the stem or they will continue to bleed. Narcissus is an example of a flower that produces a sap that is toxic to other flowers; narcissi must be conditioned in a separate bucket to other plants and the water should be changed frequently over the course of a number of hours until the sap stops emerging from the end.

Large hollow stems Delphiniums and amaryllis are examples of plants with hollow stems. Fill the stems with water, plug the ends with cotton wool and secure with an elastic band to prevent them from splitting.

Vase life

Understanding how a cut flower stays hydrated and the impediments to the stem's uptake of water can help you prolong the life of the stem once cut.

TRANSPIRATION

Water and nutrients are carried through the plant stem by vascular tissue called xylem and are transported from the roots of a plant up through the stems to the leaves and flowers by a process called transpiration. Moisture is constantly being lost from a plant through tiny holes called stomata on the undersides of the leaves, which causes more water to be drawn up from the roots and through the stems to replace it. When you see a plant wilting in response to heat, this can often be because water is not being replaced in the leaves as quickly as it is being lost in the transpiration process. When we cut a stem, we need to replace its access to water, so that the transpiration process can continue and it can remain hydrated and turgid (full of water) in the vase.

BACTERIA

Bacteria is the enemy of cut flowers; bacteria will multiply at the cut surface of the stem and block the xylem, stopping water uptake and leading to the ultimate death of the flower. This is why it is so important

to make sure that everything you use is scrupulously clean: your cutting tools, buckets and vases should all be spotless. Any vessels used to hold flowers should be clean enough to drink out of. Make sure that your cutting tools are also disinfected to ensure a clean cut and minimise any potential transfer of bacteria or disease between plants.

FLOWER FOOD VS CLEAN WATER

It is possible to buy flower food, which is basically a mix of sugars (carbohydrates) to feed the flower and bleach or a disinfectant to reduce bacterial growth. The problem is that the sugars also feed and contribute to bacterial growth.

Many studies have shown that flowers last just as long in fresh, clean water as they do in water with added flower food, provided that an effort is made to change the water in the vase every day. Always wash the vase out every time you change the water, and also trim the stem ends before replacing them in the clean vase. This three-pronged process will significantly reduce bacterial build-up in your vases and help flowers to last longer. Water that has not been changed in a week will be smelly and murky, and the slime at the bottom of stems in week-

is spotlessly clean and your flowers will last as long as it's possible for them to last.

DIRTY STEMS

Certain varieties of flowers have what florists call 'dirty' stems – the enzymes in the plant encourage rapid bacterial growth and they can sour vase water quickly. The water will certainly need to be changed every day to prevent bacteria from building up. Some of the key 'dirty' plants are: achillea, amaranthus, dahlias, marigolds, stocks, sunflowers and zinnias.

TIPS FOR VASE LIFE

There are a few other factors that can hasten the death flowers, so be sure to follow these points to care for yours once they are in the vase:

- Place the vase in a cool location out of direct sunlight – not on a sunny windowsill or above a source of heat like a radiator.
- Keep flowers away from sources of ethylene such as fruit bowls.
- Cigarette smoke contains chemicals that shorten the life of flowers.
- Never mix old flowers with new; the bacteria on the older stems will attack the new stems with vigour, causing them to die more quickly.

old water is a sure sign of bacterial growth killing off your flowers.

There are a number of synthetic products on the market that claim to help hydrate or prolong the life of your flowers once cut. But I would ask why, when you've gone to the trouble of growing lovely blooms without the use of additional chemical sprays, would you put those stems into a chemical solution once cut? Grow healthy plants, cut at the right stage, make sure that all of your equipment

Drying flowers

There has been a resurgence of interest in dried (or everlasting) flowers and for good reason – they are beautiful. In naturally air-dried flowers we capture the essence of the summer garden. While freshly cut blooms have something of an ephemeral nature, the preserving process of drying allows us to enjoy our bounty right through the cold, dark months of winter.

In a temperate climate, we know that it isn't possible to grow flowers for twelve months of the year. We also know that the imported, out-of-season bunches that we are able to purchase all year round have a significant carbon footprint. Flowers that are grown in the garden and cut and dried at the height of summer will provide a wealth of floral material for winter arranging, carrying with them the warmth and colour of summer. There are no air miles to consider, no energy used for industrial drying and no single-use plastic packaging.

Of course, not every plant is suitable for drying, and just as with fresh blooms, flowers for drying will have an optimum stage for cutting which is different for every plant. You can cut from all of the different types of plant – annuals, biennials, bulbs, perennials and woodies. And it's not only flowers that are suitable for drying – foliage, grasses, ferns, seedheads and buds can also be dried to offer a range of textures to work with. Just as with fresh flowers, you need to consider drying a range of different floral forms (see page 23) to create interesting arrangements.

Ranunculus and dahlias are good focal elements in dried arrangements (though they need careful drying to preserve the flower heads without rotting). And delphiniums make amazing dried material, providing a spike flower shape in a range of colours. *Xerochrysum bracteatum* (strawflower) is the quintessential dried flower – its little pops of colour are called 'everlastings' because they can last for years.

The garden also provides plant material that is less commonly used for drying, so don't be afraid to test anything that looks interesting! Grasses are easy to dry and add a wonderful range of textural elements. Look at developing seedheads for unusual shapes and textures – silene, veronica and gillenia all produce lovely seedheads.

Remember that bright colours of freshly cut blooms will fade and soften slightly, but if dried correctly, the flowers are not just shades of brown!

DRYING FOR FLOWER COLOUR

- *Achillea* (yarrow)
- *Acroclinium* (pink paper daisy)
- *Alchemilla* (lady's mantle)
- *Amaranthus* (amaranth)
- *Ammobium alatum* (winged everlasting)
- *Astrantia* (masterwort)
- *Centaurea cyanus* (cornflower)
- *Craspedia globosa* (drumsticks)
- *Dahlia* (dahlia)
- *Delphinium* (delphinium)
- *Delphinium consolida* (larkspur)
- *Echinops* (globe thistle)
- *Eryngium* (sea holly)
- *Tanacetum parthenium* (feverfew)
- *Gomphrena* (globe amaranth)
- *Gypsophila* (baby's breath)
- *Hydrangea* (hydrangea)
- *Lavandula* (lavender)
- *Paeonia* (peony)
- *Physalis alkekengi* (Chinese lantern)
- *Ranunculus* (Persian buttercup)
- *Rosa* (rose)
- *Limonium* (statice)
- *Xerochrysum bracteatum* (strawflower)
- *Zinnia* (zinnia)

SEEDHEADS AND TEXTURAL ELEMENTS

- *Allium* (allium)
- *Aquilegia* (columbine)
- *Astilbe* (astilbe)
- *Atriplex* (orache)
- *Avena sativa* (oat)
- *Briza* (quaking grass)
- *Calamagrostis* (feather reed-grass)
- *Chasmanthium latifolium* (northern sea oats)
- *Clematis* (clematis)
- *Cortaderia selloana* (pampas grass)
- *Crocosmia* (montbretia)
- *Daucus* (wild carrot)
- *Dipsacus* (teasel)
- *Echinacea* (coneflower)
- *Eucalyptus* (gum)
- *Filipendula* (meadowsweet)
- *Geum* (avens)
- *Gillenia* (Bowman's root)
- *Lagurus ovatus* (hare's tail grass)
- *Lepidium sativum* (garden cress)
- *Lunaria* (honesty)
- *Miscanthus* (silver grass)
- *Nigella* (love-in-a-mist)
- *Origanum* (oregano)
- *Panicum* (switch grass)
- *Papaver* (poppy)
- *Pennisetum* (fountain grass)
- *Phalaris canariensis* (canary grass)
- *Pteridium aquilinum* (bracken)
- *Salvia nemorosa* (Balkan clary)
- *Scabiosa* (scabious)
- *Setaria* (foxtail millet)
- *Silene* (campion)
- *Thlaspi* (pennycress)
- *Triticum* (wheat)
- *Veronicastrum* (culver's root)

Opposite A selection of material for drying, including *Scabiosa stellata* (starflower scabious), echinacea, helichrysum, eryngium, nigella, *Daucus carota* (wild carrot), *Avena sativa* (oat), and *Setaria italica* 'Hylander' and *S. viridis* 'Caramel' (foxtail millet 'Hylander and 'Caramel')

AIR DRYING AND EVAPORATION

Air drying is the easiest and most popular way of drying flowers at home, and evaporation works well for specific plants, but there are other techniques you can go on to explore, such as using a flower press, silica drying and dehydration.

When air drying stems there are a couple of factors to consider in order to achieve the best results. The floral material should be gathered into small bunches which will allow the air to circulate freely; the bunches should be hung upside down from hooks (or similar) to allow them to dry straight. Make sure that the bunches are bound tightly, as they will shrink once dried, but take care not to crush the stems.

The bunches should be hung somewhere dark (or in an area of low light) at room temperature. Sunlight will bleach the colour out of petals or even scorch them if the light is particularly strong; a conservatory is not a suitable space for drying. A damp atmosphere will cause your plant material to rot rather than dry, and excessive heat can cause the stems to become brittle and easily damaged. Leave to dry for around 4–6 weeks. Some larger, fleshier flowers (like peonies or roses) may take a little longer to fully dehydrate.

Once your stems are completely dry they can be wrapped in paper to protect the flowers and sealed into airtight boxes until you are ready to work with them. They can be stored for many months, but only if they are in a completely dry, airtight container as any moisture can lead to mould forming. You can reuse the small bags of silica that are often found in packing boxes to help absorb any moisture.

Evaporation is another easy method for drying and can be particularly useful for woody-stemmed plants like hydrangeas. Fill a vase with approximately 5cm (2in) of water, place the woody stems into the vase and set it somewhere that isn't too bright. The stem will drink and the water will slowly evaporate, leaving the flower head beautifully preserved and ready to use in an everlasting arrangement.

DRIED FLOWER ARRANGEMENTS

Everlasting flowers are incredibly versatile and can be used in all manner of arrangements, from traditional hand-tied bouquets and table centrepieces to a contemporary hanging installation. They also look wonderful in wreaths, which can be used to adorn a wall or door all year long (see page 153).

A gentle blow from a hair-dryer on the lowest setting will help to keep your dried arrangements dust free. Remember that arrangements exposed to strong light will eventually bleach to a straw colour, but by that time you will be drying a new batch of fresh flowers.

Floral displays

Creating floral displays from flowers you have grown is an incredibly satisfying experience. It is a joy to be able to gift your flowers to friends and family, to share the pleasure and beauty of your homegrown blooms, and also to fill your home with nature's colours and shapes. If you haven't tried flower arranging before, it can be a daunting prospect – it's a discipline that's traditionally filled with techniques and rules – but there are a few simple methods you can learn to help you make the most of your flowers.

A NOTE ON FLORAL FOAM

In recent years, traditional floristry has made great use of floral foam which was developed by Smithers-Oasis in the 1950s. Floral foam transformed the floristry industry as it is incredibly easy to use, can be carved into any shape and provides both hydration and support to flowers in arrangements. It became the go-to product for professionals and amateurs, with little thought for its production, disposal and environmental impact.

Floral foam is a single-use plastic product that only has a negative impact on our natural environment. It is neither recyclable nor biodegradable. It is produced using a number of dangerous chemicals including phenol and formaldehyde and should only be disposed of into landfill where it will never break down. It can be cut and shaved to form any shape desired, but a mask should always be worn while cutting to prevent the inhalation of tiny particles which can cause respiratory problems. Foam particles present yet another problem by contributing to the microplastic pollution crisis: when soaked in water, they are washed down into drains, enter watercourses and ultimately disperse, ending up in marine environments such as rivers and oceans. A 2019 report showed that they are extremely toxic to aquatic life.

Newer 'bio' floral foam products have been shown to be just as harmful; they do not actually biodegrade fully and cannot be composted. Some research has shown that they can leach higher levels of toxic chemicals into the natural environment than conventional foam products.

Frankly, there is no place for floral foam in floristry; an industry that celebrates the beauty of the natural world cannot continue to perpetuate the use of these damaging products. Luckily, there is absolutely no need to use floral foam for your arrangements as there are other simple techniques that are just as effective.

SUPPORTING ARRANGEMENTS

Before the introduction of foam an array of techniques were available to floral arrangers. Flowers always last longer when the stems are placed directly into water anyway, and you can create your own armatures to support the stems using different materials for different types of floral display.

Kenzan / pin frog This is a Japanese device that has been used for centuries in the floral art of ikebana. It is a weighted brass plate set with upright pins which grip the base of the stems and hold them in place in an arrangement. Pin frogs will last for many years and come in a variety of sizes and shapes to fit different types of vessels. They can be used in combination with a chicken wire armature in large vases to provide extra support if necessary.

Flower frogs Also known as cage frogs, hairpin frogs and pin frogs, these come in all sizes and materials: metal, glass, ceramic and plastic. They can be used for years and can be placed into vases to provide support for flower stems.

Chicken wire or copper mesh Either wire or mesh can be used to create armatures to fit any size of vessel or to create the framework for installations, which can be packed with moss depending on the type of construction. This is a versatile way of supporting

flowers and the wire and mesh can be reused for years, though they will eventually biodegrade by corrosion.

Moss This is a renewable material that can be used to fill wire shapes and to help hold the water to keep your flowers hydrated. It is widely used and can be bound to a wire or willow frame for wreath making. It is also useful to hide the mechanics of arrangements. Just ensure that you purchase it from a recognised supplier of sustainably gathered moss. If you have a lawn, you can rake out the moss for your own use every year. Please don't ever collect it from the wild.

Tape A simple grid made out of sticky florists' pot tape can be placed over the top of your vessel to provide support for stems. It can be an easy and useful solution for vases with oddly-shaped openings. Take care to conceal any tape around the rim with foliage or flowers.

Pliable branches Willow or hazel can be used to create an armature or framework for arrangements or large bouquets. Be aware that branches can increase bacterial growth if submerged in water, so this method is useful for one-off events, but less successful for fresh designs that you would like to last for a week. Pliable woody stems (such as hazel or willow) are great bases for wreaths as an alternative to wire frames. Floral foam wreath bases should be avoided altogether.

ASYMMETRIC LATE SPRING PASTEL ARRANGEMENT

This arrangement uses a large vintage confit pot with a wide neck to display the soft, pastel blooms of late spring. In such a large vessel it is necessary to use both a kenzen or frog and a chicken wire armature to hold the stems in place.

- Secure a weighted kenzan or frog in the base of the vessel.
- Cut and fold a piece of chicken wire into a rough ball shape, making sure you have two layers for the stems to pass through. Push this into the vessel so it is wedged about half way down the container. Fill the vessel with water.
- Start by selecting your structural foliage material. For this arrangement I've used viburnum, pittosporum and cornus to create an asymmetrical shape.
- Insert your foliage to create three points of a triangle with the high and middle points to each side and the lowest point towards the front of the vessel – this gives balance to the asymmetry. Silver birch has been used to trail over the edges of the vase to soften the edges.
- Select and place your focal flowers. Start in the centre and then work outwards looking at where your eye naturally wants to rest while regarding the arrangement. The rounded shapes of anemones and ranunculus in late spring are ideal for this purpose.

- In an asymmetrical arrangement, supporting flowers can be used to extend and enhance the asymmetrical lines. Here I've used camassia to extend beyond the line of the foliage. The lightness of the supporting alliums also emphasise the asymmetrical line and they are a contrast to the heavier, petal-filled ranunculus flower heads.
- Add your filler material. I've used white and pale mauve *Hesperis matronalis* (sweet rocket) to add a frothy contrast to the round and spike shapes used so far.
- Lastly, insert your textural and airy elements. Dancing silene and nepeta add movement and a delicate lightness to this spring arrangement.

MIDSUMMER MEADOW CENTREPIECE

This small arrangement takes inspiration from flower-filled summer meadows. It incorporates varieties such as nigella, early annual grasses and poppy seedheads to evoke a sense of a wild garden. Think about where an arrangement like this could be displayed. For example, if it is for a table centrepiece, it will be seen from all angles and the stem lengths shouldn't be so long that guests struggle to see each other across a dining table; but if it is going to be displayed on a mantelpiece, it will only be viewed from the front, so you can incorporate longer stems and be more adventurous with the shape. This sort of arrangement is also easy to create using dried material – make up the mechanics in the same way, just don't fill the inner container with water.

- Fold chicken wire into a pillow shape and place into a reused watertight container, securing the top with floral tape.
- Insert the watertight container into the decorative wooden vessel and fill it with water.
- Cover the top of the chicken wire with moss to disguise the armature within the vessel.
- This arrangement requires a lighter form of greenery than woody-stemmed foliage, so think about using leaves from herbaceous plants to soften the edges of the vessel. Insert the stems through the moss into the chicken wire frame of the inner container using a bamboo skewer to push a hole through the moss if necessary.
- This particular style of arranging doesn't follow conventional rules using structure/focals/filler. Start to build the arrangement, letting the material lead your creativity.

- Cut the stems of your flowers and grasses to varying heights and insert randomly into the vessel. The aim is to evoke the essence of a self-seeded annual border or a natural wildflower meadow. Shorter lengths can be inserted around the perimeter of the container.
- Remember not to pack the stems too tightly – the negative space between them is equally important, and you want to create a sense of light and movement rather than a dense, static display.
- Make sure that none of the mechanics are visible once you have finished.

LATE SUMMER BOUQUET

This is an example of a loose, garden-gathered bouquet rather than a tight, formal hand-tie. A good balance of different flower shapes adds interest – round heads, spikes, sprays of smaller filler flowers – and the bouquet should feel like something that has just been scooped up from the garden.

- Before you start to make the bouquet, prepare the material by stripping two thirds of the foliage away from each stem, leaving just a third at the top. Use an odd number of each variety selected – threes, fives or sevens – as this will produce a more satisfying and balanced arrangement than an even number of stems.

- Lay each individual variety out on the table in front of you – this will make it easier to select each stem as you construct the bouquet. Leave the airy elements to the side as these delicate stems can be added at the end.

- Start by selecting a focal flower which will sit at the centre of the bouquet. Then add a couple of stems of supporting and filler flowers. Once you are happy with the centre, you can begin to build the bouquet.

- If you are right-handed, hold the bouquet in your left hand while adding blooms with your right, and vice-versa if you are left-handed. With the bouquet held loosely about halfway down the stems, start to add the remaining stems at a 30-degree angle. Turn the bouquet clockwise in the left hand each time you add a

couple of stems. Take care to check that your bouquet looks balanced as you turn it and add further stems.

- Always make sure that you only turn the bouquet one way and that your stems are all laying in the same direction. This way you create a loose spiral of stems that will sit neatly in a vase – a particularly important consideration if you are going to be using a glass vessel.

- Once you've incorporated most of the stems, insert the delicate airy elements to add movement and finish off the bouquet. Cut all of the stems to the same length at a 45-degree angle.

- Tie off the bouquet with a piece of string or raffia. To do this, double over a length of string and, holding the loop, grasp the loose stem ends and pull them through to secure the stems. Lay the bouquet down, split the strings and wrap them in opposite directions around the back of the bouquet. Bring the strings around to the front, tie them tightly together in a double knot and cut off the excess.

- Wrap in paper and place into water until you are ready to gift it to someone to enjoy!

DAHLIA ABUNDANCE

A large vessel is perfect for displaying an abundance of dahlias in autumn. No mechanics here, just careful placement of the stems to showcase the variety of dahlia shapes and sizes, as well as textural autumn grasses and foliage.

- Choose a vessel made of an opaque material so that the stems cannot be seen. Half fill the vase with water. I have used restricted colours within the same tonal palette to create a sense of continuity.
- Start by placing your structural foliage in the vase. Here, the arching stems of abelia create a frame and the small leaves and flowers will be a foil to the larger dahlia flower heads. Make sure that the stems criss-cross in the vase to provide a framework that will lock together once further stems are inserted.
- Add your larger focal dahlias. Cut the stems at different lengths to create interest. Place a bloom at the rim of the vase just slightly off-centre to start, then arrange the others around that. No hard and fast rules – we want to create a feeling of abundance, but make sure you leave some room between stems so they are not crammed together, as this could damage them.
- Insert the smaller flower heads to add another layer of interest.
- Sparkling grasses can be added into gaps to bring lightness and movement to what would otherwise be quite a static arrangement.

DRIED FLORAL WREATH

How do you use your bounty of dried summer flowers? You create a gorgeous wreath, of course, full of texture and a sweet reminder of the summer garden.

- A dried flower wreath can be constructed using either a wire, metal or wood frame for the base.
- Select the floral material you would like to use. Think about incorporating a range of different flower shapes and textures to create layers of interest. For example, helichrysum, eryngium and nigella seedheads for round shapes, wheat and veronica seedheads for spikes, and briza, oats and geum seedheads for movement. See page 136 for good options.
- Prepare the material by stripping excess leaves and cutting into short lengths around 10–15cm (4–6in) long. Sort each variety into bundles.
- You can use florist reel wire or raffia to attach the dried material to the frame. Wrap it around the frame at your starting point, securing one end by twisting the wire or tying the raffia in a knot. I like to use wire as it keeps taut throughout the construction.
- Take a stem of each variety to create a small bunch that incorporates all of the shapes and textures. Lay the bunch on the frame and bring your wire/raffia around to attach the stems. I like to wrap around twice to ensure the stems are secure. Don't wrap tightly just below the flower heads – make sure that you leave a little bit of stem above the wire/raffia to allow for small adjustments as you go.
- Take a second small bunch and lay the heads across the stems of the first bunch and secure, ensuring that you are laying the bunches in the same direction. As you continue to add bunches you will see a consistent design begin to build. Using the same material throughout creates a sense of rhythm and balance.
- Continue to build the wreath all the way around the base for a traditional look. For something more contemporary, try covering 30–50 per cent of the base. Remember that the weight of a partially covered wreath will be heaviest where the material is attached and that this will affect how it hangs.
- To finish, attach the final small bunch, then wrap the wire/raffia around the stems a couple of times, threading it through the loops and tying off to secure. On a full wreath the stem ends will be tucked under the heads of the first bunch, but on a partially covered base, you can cover the exposed ends with something like a wrap of raffia or ribbon.
- Hang your wreath somewhere dry and keep it dust free by blowing it with a hair-dryer on the lowest setting.

Page numbers in *italic* indicate a caption or illustration. Those in **bold** indicate a main entry. Common herbs are mainly given as their common names; those of other plants are given as their Latin names with cross-reference from their common names.

Further resources

A Guide to Floral Mechanics
Sarah Diligent and William Mazuch
agtfm.com

Sustainable Floristry Network
sustainablefloristry.org

The Sustainable Cut-Flowers Project
sustainableflowers.coventry.domains

Flowers From The Farm
flowersfromthefarm.co.uk

Follow @prairiegirlflowers on Instagram for the
Sustainability Sunday series

Acknowledgments

Deepest thanks and love to Robert, my husband, who is
always there to support me no matter what. And to our
children, Leia and Rowan, who are always there with love
and chat to cheer me on.

Special thanks must go to Sherry and Nick Amis whose kindness
over the years has allowed my flower obsession to bloom.
They took a chance and allowed a woman with a flower-filled
dream to take over the field next to their house – I hope I never
give them cause to regret that decision!

To Harriet Smithson, my flower-farming confidant, thank you
for your endless support and dedication to the sustainable
flower movement. Always a voice of sense and reason.

To all of the local, seasonal flower growers across the globe
who are forging a path towards a more sustainable future for
the floristry industry – this is the time for real change. To Erin
Benzakein of Floret Flower Farm, thank you for sharing your
knowledge and being such an inspiration to so many of us.
To Becky Feasby of Prairie Girl Flowers, you've shown us how
to be fearless in the face of adversity and change. And thanks
to Rita Feldmann of the Sustainable Floristry Network whose
vision of the future of floristry will help guide the way.

Finally, thank you to Zena Alkayat and the teams at Bloom
and Frances Lincoln for offering me the opportunity to fulfil
a long-held dream.

Think global, act local.